GENESIS
Rooted in Relationship

Let the word of Christ dwell in you richly as you teach and admonish
one another with all wisdom, and as you sing psalms, hymns and spiritual
songs with gratitude in your hearts to God (Colossians 3:16).

Prepared by Laine Rosin

Edited by Thomas J. Doyle

CPH™
SAINT LOUIS

Editorial assistant: Phoebe Wellman

2 3 4 5 6 7 8 9 10   VP   03 02 01 00 99

Contents

Introduction

Alex Haley's *Roots* was one of television's biggest blockbusters. Many people trace coats of arms and family trees in order to reach into their past, hoping to discover something about themselves and their own roots.

Perhaps the interest is due partly to rootlessness. The family unit is no longer a part of a functioning, clanlike whole. It has become an enclave in a hostile world. Detached from their roots, many families seem to lack depth. They move about from place to place, muddle along, and turn to professionals and "self-help" books for the guidance and support that the extended family used to provide. And often, unable to sustain their integrity in the face of isolation, the family relationships themselves break down.

In this study of the book of **Genesis** we find the answers to the age-old quest of humanity—the search for identity. We find not the names of all of our ancestors, but the ultimate family tree—our deepest roots. Here in **Genesis** we have God's inspired account of the very origin of our human race and the relationships that characterize human existence. Our study of **Genesis** will not concentrate on what it says about how the world came to be, but on what it says about who we are and why we are—our roots. We will explore what **Genesis** has to say about the reasons we act the way we do—our relationships. The study will examine the truth—our real roots are in God, and our broken relationships with Him and with each other result from the fall into sin. Most important, this study will note that the book of **Genesis** is a story of the beginnings of God's acting to choose and save His people and the beginning of His promises to send a Savior, Jesus Christ.

For those who desire to discuss the detailed account of what **Genesis** records about the creation of the world, we recommend a separate session at the beginning of the class.

In these lessons we will fix our attention on God and His creatures—that great drama of creation, sin, separation, judgment, and salvation. The events that happened so long ago still have great implications for us today.

Part I

Beginnings

Lesson 1

In the Beginning . . . (Genesis 1–2)

Introduction

"Who Am I?"

One hundred years ago the question would not have been asked. People knew who they were, what family they belonged to, what nation or area they came from, even the plot of ground where they would be buried. Now we seem to have lost our sense of belonging. "Who am I?" the young ask. "What am I and what am I worth? Where am I going?"

Surely part of the reason for the searching is that often we have lost sight of our real roots. We constantly forget who we are in relationship to God, to God's world, and to one another. A study of **Genesis 1–2** reveals to us our origins—our roots in God and relationship to Him. This portion of God's Word sets forth identity and the basis of our relationship to others.

Overview

Genesis 1—the beginning. The stage is set for the drama—the God/human drama, the Creator/creature drama. It is a drama in which God is the central actor. He acts; He creates. Then later in the book, it is this great actor—God—who condemns and acts to punish, then forgives and acts to save. In this chapter we see Him as the universal God, spinning out the reaches of the heavens and the earth by His creating Word, beginning time and life and space and, finally, creating this unique creature—man.

Chapter 2 gives a more intimate view of God and a more detailed account of the creation of man. Here we see God the giver: giving life, like a potter to his clump of clay; giving the world and dominion over it to His hand-formed creation; and creating a woman for His created man as a suitable helpmate and partner. And here is man—God's created man—sharing life by the hand of God with this woman.

Focus 1: Roots

1. What do **Genesis 1:26–27; 2:4–8;** and **2:21–22** tell us about the roots of humanity? about our own roots? Does it matter? Does the fact that we are from God—created by His loving hand—have an effect on our lives now?

In **2:7** God breathes into man the breath of life. What does this say about life as a gift from God? In what sense do we "own" our life? Do we have the right to take life? any life?

2. What do **Genesis 1:28–31** and **2:8–14** tell us about our roots *in the world?* In what way are we different from animals?

3. In **Genesis 2:15–17** we are told that God set up boundaries for Adam. What was Adam not to do? What does this say about the uniqueness of man in comparison to the other creatures? What does this tell us about our roots?

Focus 2: Relationships

1. Go back to **Genesis 1:26–27; 2:4–8;** and **2:21–22.** How would you describe the relationship between God and His creature, man? What does

it mean to be created in the "image of God"? How is the relationship between God and man unique? What does it say about our basic relationship to God? How does being separated from one's roots in God show itself in people?

2. Read **Genesis 1:28–30; 2:4–9;** and **2:18–20.** Remember that, in the Old Testament world, to name someone or something often meant to have rule over that person or thing. What do the verses say about man's relationship to the world in which he was placed? Do we still have that kind of dominion over creation?

Does dominion include the right to destroy? How does this concept of dominion fit with the truth that life is a gift of God?

3. Read **Genesis 2:20–24.** What unique relationship is indicated between man and woman? In what sense is the relationship different from that between man and all other creatures? What does the emphasis on oneness **(v. 24)** tell us about the marriage relationship?

Creation Now

1. Some people complain that they often feel "worthless." Worthlessness can take the form of self-hatred. Self-hatred is always destructive. More important, obsession with one's self, even self-hatred, is a kind of inverted pride, which falls under God's condemnation. Self-hatred leads to acts of anger, violence, self-punishment, and the disintegration of all personal relationships. What does **Genesis 1–2** say about our worth? What unique worth are we shown in this portion of Scripture?

How are Christians better able to deal with the sense of worthlessness than those who see humanity as the end product of an evolution?

What does God's willingness to offer His only Son in terrible death on the cross for this creature of His tell us about His relationship to us?

2. After reading these chapters of **Genesis,** and also **Ephesians 5:21–33** and **1 Peter 3:1–7,** how would you characterize the God-ordained relationship between husbands and wives?

What does it mean for wives to be subject to their husbands?

Read **Galatians 3:28.** In what way are husbands and wives "one"?

What is necessary to create a truly "God-intended" marriage relationship? Is it possible to create that kind of relationship separate from a relationship rooted in God?

Why is the message of Christ's forgiveness particularly important to those who are married?

Lesson 2

Something Happened (Genesis 3–4)

Introduction

Creation took place a long time ago, and centuries later we still feel exiled from Eden. We long for Eden's beauty, harmony, and perfection. Politically and personally we try to create it for ourselves in "great societies" or "new world orders" or "perfect vacation spots." But that perfection eludes us. In fact, perfection is gone. It no longer exists in the world or in us.

Life is not a harmony of beauty, accomplishment, approval, and success. It is filled, as well, with sorrow, disappointment, failure, pain, and finally death. The battle rages, and on our own we cannot overcome.

Here the book of **Genesis** touches our very selves. Here we see the first step—the root step that started humankind on that lonely trek through the ages, separated from the Creator, even now continuing to pass on the guilt of that separation and its resulting death to each person—to each one of us.

Overview

God made everything good—man destroyed it. Adam blamed Eve; Eve blamed the serpent; but the result was the same. The boundary was crossed; the choice was made; perfection was lost.

Such a simple act—just take the fruit and be like God, know good and evil. But the aftermath of that act still torments us and marks us for death. It was so easy, and it is still so easy, to go one's own way, to seek to be God, to try to overcome life on one's own. And when we fail, it is easy to point the finger at others, at the devil, or even at God.

The destruction that resulted manifests itself in all areas of life. The roots of mankind in God were ripped free; the perfect relationship of man to woman and person to person was set in the process of continual disintegration. The human family became a family of creatures set on a course of self-destruction. So Adam and Eve's children are no longer born in the image of God but in the image of their parents and separated from God. Cain and Abel live out the destruction they inherit, as Cain violently kills his brothers. And so they die, caught in the web of sin that will not let them free.

Focus 1: Roots—Who Is to Blame?

1. Was the tree at fault? The tree was called the "tree of the knowledge of good and evil." Look at **Genesis 2:9; 2:16–17; 3:1–3;** and **3:22–24.** What was unique about this tree?

Was the tree evil? Did God create anything evil?

Why was the eating of the fruit of the tree destructive?

2. Was the serpent at fault? Who was this serpent? Is he named in this portion of Scripture?

Who does **Revelation 20:2** say he was? What interest did he have in getting Adam and Eve to disobey God? Did he have power over them?

What picture of Satan do we have in **1 Peter 5:8?** In what sense was this serpent/lion at fault? What punishment does he receive in **3:15?**

3. Was Eve at fault? What does **3:6–13** say Eve was seeking in the fruit of the tree? Did she find it?

Why couldn't she blame the snake? What was her punishment according to **3:16?**

4. Was Adam at fault? Why did he join Eve in her disobedience?

Why could he not blame Eve for his mistake, and what does **3:17–19** say his punishment was?

Focus 2: Relationships—What Happened as a Result?

1. What were the initial consequences of sin according to **3:7–13?** How does sin still affect our lives?

2. What were the physical consequences of the fall according to **3:14–19?** How are these consequences reflected in our present relationships?

3. Study **Genesis 4:1–10.** How is the result of sin acted out in these people? What do Cain's words in **4:9** say about the breakdown of human relationships? How are the words repeated today?

4. Read **Genesis 4:17–24.** How do these descendants of Cain demonstrate the continuing breakdown of their relationship to God? How are they like the people of our world today?

Creation Now

1. The picture in **Genesis 3–4** is devastating. What hope does **3:15** bring to this seemingly hopeless situation?

Why is this passage called the first promise of the Gospel? What does this promise tell us about the nature of God?

Why is it necessary that we study the story of creation and the fall in connection with Christ's death and resurrection?

How can the misuse of this portion of Scripture cause despair and unbelief, rather than lead people to a closer relationship with God?

What is the "right" way to see ourselves and others reflected in the account of the fall? What do **3:21–24** and **4:25–26** tell us about God's concern for His fallen creatures?

2. Sometimes people attempt to excuse their sins and mistakes by saying, "I couldn't help it"; It's just something born in me"; "The devil made me do it"; "I guess it's a weakness I inherited from my parents." Read **Romans 5:12, 15–19.** What is the result of Adam's sin for all of us who have come after him?

Does our inherited or original sin excuse what we do?

When God sets aside our sin, does He simply excuse it? How does the death of Jesus on the cross eliminate any possibility of "excusing" sin?

What does God's forgiveness say about the way we tend to excuse the sin of others and refuse to forgive those who have hurt us?

3. Why is it so difficult to take responsibility for our own actions? Why do we often blame others for what we do, seeking to avoid personal blame?

Those who don't believe in Christ have no solution to the problem of guilt, except to try to avoid it or escape it by putting the guilt on someone else. Why is it possible for those of us who believe in Jesus to be free from the sense of guilt that destroys so many?

What gift has God given us that allows us to acknowledge our own evil and to ask Him for forgiveness?

Lesson 3

Beginning Again (Genesis 6–11)

Introduction

Some people tend to slip through life with "just in case" faith. When the chips are down and things get rough—or, God forbid, they face death—they get out their faith, conveniently kept for the occasion, and use it: "Lord, help me!" They cash in on the spiritual "insurance policy."

Noah was allowed no such luxury. He was required to act on his faith. But his response to the Word of God was not simply taking his turn making an evangelism call nor a slight increase in his offering envelope. He had to build a boat. And what a boat! Actually, it was an ark—a huge, monumental craft, the likes of which had not been seen before. And Noah built it because he believed the Word of God.

Noah built that great boat on dry land, with nary a puddle in sight nor a cloud in the sky. For years he worked in faith, trusting that God would stand by His Word and act on His promised judgment and salvation.

People must have laughed at Noah—silly old man with his "white elephant" ark. Surely they laughed and laughed—until it started to rain.

Overview

Chapter 6 makes it clear—things did not improve after the Cain and Abel incident. Man, it seems, was unable to learn the lesson of obedience and unable to maintain a relationship with God.

And so the story is repeated—the Adam and Eve story with a bigger and more diverse cast. But this encounter between God and His creatures takes on an added dimension. In the Adam and Eve event, the cause of sin is disobedient pride, the result of sin is judgment, and the judgment is countered by the announcement of the grace of God in the first Gospel promise in **3:15.** The story of Noah contains all of those elements with the added feature of Noah himself, a man who "found favor" with God **(6:8).** Like other righteous men in the Scriptures, Noah is a chosen one, selected to be the conveyer of God's saving action.

Chapter 7 tells us of God's act of saving through Noah, whose ark-building act of faith saves his family and a "remnant" of the first creation.

But just as exclusion from the garden, the promise of the Savior to come, and the marking of Cain did not overcome the sin in man, neither did this great flood.

Noah succeeds at building an ark but fails at being righteous. **Chapter 9:20–29** reveals how human Noah was. He gets drunk and curses his son because of his son's indiscretion. The hero does heroic deeds but fails his own children.

Once again, man's sin is made eminently clear. The descendants of Noah, who elect to set up a civilization in Babel **(11:1–9),** follow in the footsteps of Adam and Eve. Repeated again is the arrogance of humankind. As Eve wanted to be like God, so these people want to "reach" God with their presumptuous building. And again they fall under the judgment of God and are scattered.

But amid the judgments and creature's failures, amid the gloomy picture of destruction, the changeless light of the grace of God shines through. There is a unique promise given to Noah and his descendants: God will never again destroy the world with a flood. The promise is sealed with a rainbow **(9:8–17).**

The section of **Genesis** called "beginnings" comes to an end, setting the stage for other judgments and other promises; other choosings and other victories; other signs and wonders; other times when God saves His people in spite of themselves, because of Himself and His steadfast love.

Focus 1: Roots

1. Skim **chapter 6.** In what ways is Noah like Adam? In what sense is Noah a new Adam? Read **9:20–28.** In what way did Noah fail like Adam? In what sense are we "righteous" as Noah? Read **Hebrews 11:7.**

2. Read **11:1–9.** How is the story like that of the fall in **Genesis 3?** What similar elements in the stories can you find? How is God's response similar?

Are people any different today than at the time of Babel?

3. Use your Bibles, Bible history books, and Bible dictionaries to compare Noah, Abraham, David, Moses, and Jeremiah. Answer these questions:
   a. How were they chosen?
   b. In what way were they "righteous"?
   c. How did they respond to God's choosing them?
   d. How were they vehicles of the promises of God?
   e. In what way did they demonstrate their sinfulness?

Focus 2: Relationships
1. Read **6:5–12.** What do the verses say about man's relationship to God and to his fellow man at Noah's time? In what way would Noah feel very much at home in our world today? Has anything changed?

2. It is interesting to go through the data about the ark: how big it was; how it looked; how many animals it would hold; how much food Noah needed, and the like. But the story speaks most clearly about God's relationship to His created beings. What does the flood say about God's attitude toward sin? Does He take it seriously?

Why is it so difficult for people to accept the truth that God hates sin?

3. Even more important for us as Christians: What is God's relationship to His "chosen" people? In what sense is Noah chosen? Does he seek God?

In what way are we chosen?

If Noah's faith task was to build an ark, what is our faith task?

In what respects is the way God deals with Noah similar to the way He deals with us through Jesus Christ?

4. God's dealing with His people is often summarized by the word *covenant* (sometimes translated "testament"). Read these passages: **Genesis 9:9; 17:1–8; Psalm 89:3–4; Galatians 3:17; Hebrews 8:6; 12:24.** What do they tell you about God's relationship to His people?

What was a covenant? Why is it a repeated theme?

In what way did Jesus bring a "new covenant"?

Creation Now

1. Read **1 Peter 3:18–22.** Peter makes a connection between the flood and Baptism. How does the flood correspond to Baptism?

What elements are there in the account of the flood that are similar to your Baptism?

How do the themes of sin, judgment, choosing, saving, washing clean, covenant, and promise apply to you in Baptism?

What is the good news for those who are received into His kingdom through Baptism?

2. We are good at excusing sin. We tend to overlook the sin and evil that are done. We make excuses for sinners, blaming their environment, their parents, or their social status. How does the story of God's dealing with people in the flood emphasize that God indeed takes sin seriously?

Why is it important for us to realize the seriousness of our sin?

How does the message of the death and resurrection of Jesus lose its meaning for those who do not remember that God rejects and judges sin?

Part II

Patriarchal History

Lesson 4

The Father of the Nation
(Genesis 11:31–14:24)

Introduction

Abram is 75 years old, wealthy, minding his own business. He has no children, but he can't complain. He has a beautiful wife and a devoted nephew. What more could he ask?

And then . . . the choosing finger of God moves over the people of Abram's time and comes to rest on this son of Terah, living in peace in Haran.

"Go!" says the voice of God. "Go to the land I will show you."

And how does Abram respond? "Where? Where do you want me to go? How will I get there? How much will it cost? I have too many things going on here now. I'm too old to move around. I've done enough, haven't I?"

No, that is not what happened. The Bible just says, "So Abram left, as the Lord had told him" **(12:4).**

Would we do the same? What would we say? What do we say to another command to go? What about the time Jesus said, "Go and make disciples of all nations" **(Matthew 28:19)?** What do we say to that?

Overview

In this portion of Scripture the story of God's relationship to His creature begins to narrow. From the mass of humankind who continue to fail to follow Him, God selects a chosen people, and He starts with the "father of many"—Abraham (earlier called Abram).

It is a good start. God gets instant response from His chosen man. "Go," God says. And Abram goes.

Abram has a strong side. He shows it when he seeks to obey this God who told him to go. As a response to a magnificent promise to be the father of a nation that will inherit a promised land, Abram builds an altar and sacrifices to God as he should.

But Abram has his weak side too. Threatened by famine, he runs to Egypt and protects his skin by passing off his beautiful wife as his sister (**12:10–16**). The perfect hero has not yet arrived.

In spite of his occasional bouts with weakness of faith, Abram remains a remarkable man. In **13:8–13** he shows his generosity to his nephew. In **13:14–18** God repeats His covenant promise to Abram—a promise of land and innumerable descendants.

Abram gets involved. He enters the struggles of the peoples of his land. In **chapter 14** he becomes a kind of rescuer of the people in his area. It is not the last time he will act in behalf of the people of Sodom and Gomorrah.

The section ends with a curious encounter with a priest/king named Melchizedek.

Focus 1: Roots

1. Read **12:7–9** and **13:14–17.** Why are these passages important roots for the people of Israel even today?

Read also **John 8:31–59.** Why was their root in Abraham important to the Jews at Jesus' time?

In what sense did Jesus claim to be greater than Abraham? In what way are our spiritual roots in Abraham?

2. Beginning with this event and through the rest of the Scriptures, the biblical events center in the land of Canaan (Palestine), even up to the time of Jesus. Why was this country chosen? What was it, in its location and

population, that made it central in the acting of God among the people?

Focus 2: Relationships

1. Refer to your discussion of covenant in session 3. Read **Genesis 12:1–3, 7;** and **13:14–17.** Also read **Galatians 3:16.** Through whom did God fulfill the promise given to Abraham? What marks this as a covenant?

What are God's promises?

What is Abram's response in each case?

How is the covenant with Abram similar to the covenant God made with us through Jesus Christ?

How might Abram's response to God model our response to God's love for us in Jesus?

2. Abram was a "chosen one." Refer to your study of the chosen ones of God in session 3. Compare Abram to the men listed there, using the same questions. How was he chosen?

How was he "righteous"?

What was his response?

How did God use Abram to share His promises with others?

How did Abram fail?

3. Abram shows remarkable goodness in his relationship with God (12:4) and with others (13:8–13; 14:20–24). In what sense would one call Abram a "man of faith"? If he lived today, would we consider him remarkable?

In what way are the themes of obedience, worship, kindness, and unselfishness repeated by other faithful people in the Bible? by Jesus?

4. Among the most difficult and puzzling passages in **Genesis** is the account of Abram's meeting with Melchizedek in **14:17–20. Hebrews 7:1–28** and **Psalm 110:4** identify this Melchizedek as a type, or forerunner, of Christ. Look at the passages and try to explain what the author of Hebrews is telling us about our relationship with God through his explanation of the meaning of Melchizedek's appearance to Abram.

Creation Now

1. Read **12:10–19.** What does this somewhat unflattering story of Abraham say to us?

How do the elements from the beginning of **Genesis**—sin, judgment, choosing, and salvation—fit into the story of Abram here?

What does the account say about our being chosen and our failures?

Does our failure to live up to God's standard of behavior make it impossible for Him to use us in His service?

How does this account speak to those who try to excuse themselves from service to God by saying they are not "good" enough? What "goodness" did Abram, and do we, have that God can use?

2. Like Noah, Abram is required to act on his faith. Like Noah, he receives a revelation from God that demands a response. He must not only hear, but he must do. He must get up and go. **Hebrews 11:8–9** attributes Abram's ability to respond to his faith. Is it necessary that our faith *do* something in order to really be faith?

Is there such a thing as faith that does not act? What does **James 2** say about that kind of faith?

Make a list of, and discuss, the kinds of things that our faith motivates us to do in service to God. In what way are we obligated to do them?

Do our activities lend anything to our salvation? Are they necessary? In what way are they necessary?

Faith-life is a response to the goodness of God in Jesus Christ. As with Noah and Abraham, it is our active response to the commands of God that gives evidence of our faith. "Let your light shine before men," Jesus says, "that they may see your good deeds and praise your Father in heaven" **(Matthew 5:16).**

Lesson 5

Some Laughable Promises (Genesis 15–20)

Introduction

What is Abraham doing? He seems to be contending with God. He hears the promises and asks for proof. He listens to God's covenant gifts and laughs. He understands God's promise that he will be the father of a great nation, but when it does not happen quickly enough, he takes matters into his own hands. He listens to God's pronouncement of judgment upon the sinful cities of Sodom and Gomorrah, and he argues with God—tries to talk Him out of it. It seems strange to us.

At times we would like to talk with God too, even contend with Him. We would like to see a sign or two and hear His promises more clearly spelled out; we would like the blessings to come a little faster; we would like to bargain with God when He doesn't run the world or our life the way we think He should. But we can't seem to get close enough to God for all of that.

How does Abraham keep close to God? He talks to Him like a partner or friend. Why does God at times seem distant to us?

It is strange that it should be that way. We have the assurance of God's close involvement in our lives more clearly than Abraham did. We have seen God take on our very own flesh and then die our death and promise us life.

And yet when we speak to Him, we are sometimes tentative and unsure. If only we could trust like Abraham.

Overview

This part of the book of **Genesis** is a revelation about a man and his family, and not a very flattering one at that. Abram and his own are shown not as "heroes of faith," but as failing and faltering human beings. They doubt, laugh at God, manipulate and mistreat one another, lie, deceive, and in many ways demonstrate their clear connection with Adam and Eve.

But what is remarkable about this section is not what it says about Abram and the others, but what it says about God. Some of the ongoing revelations of God in relationship to His people are begun in this part of **Genesis**.

Here is God, not off in the distant heavens, but intimately involved in the life of His chosen. Here is God, judging sin **(chapter 19)** and yet demonstrating such long-suffering patience with His people as to almost be talked out of destroying the evil He had determined to eliminate **(18:26–32)**. Here is the patient God, repeating over and over again the promise to Abraham, performing signs, and giving a seal of the covenant in circumcision **(chapters 15, 17–18)**. Surely here is the "Father" God, loving Abraham and Sarah so much that He puts up with their laughter of scorn at His promises and their insistence on doing things their own way.

In each event Abraham and his family are the doers, but God is still in control. Everything is under His magnificent control. Even though Abraham cannot believe it; even though he is not patient with God's giving; even though Abraham cannot accept God's judgment and tries to talk God out of it; even though Lot only reluctantly leaves the cities of sin, carrying the sinfulness he has left with him into an incestuous relationship with his daughters; even though Abraham still staggers, protecting his own neck by again passing his wife off as his sister—God controls. God acts and gives and loves and forgives these frail beings; these creatures of His hand; these sure descendants of Adam and Eve; these chosen people.

Focus 1: Roots

1. Surely the roots of our sinfulness become clearer in these chapters. Read **15:2; 16:3–4, 6; 17:17; 18:12; 19:16, 26, 33;** and **20:11.** What kinds of sinful weakness do these people show?

Are they any different from people today? How is it possible for those whom God has chosen as His own to act in these ways?

Does God excuse them? Does He forgive them?

2. In spite of the sins, God reveals His patience with these sinners and repeats His promise of a Savior. God reveals His love totally in Jesus Christ, through whom God fulfilled His promise to save mankind. What evidence of God's patient love do you find in **15:1; 17:2–8; 18:26–33; 19:16;** and **20:6–7?**

3. The roots of our evil are very deep. Read the account of Sodom and Gomorrah in **19:1–29.** What is similar to the flood?

What events of judgment, salvation, sin, and promise do you find in both events?

What does the account say again about God's attitude toward sin?

Focus 2: Relationships
1. This section reaffirms that God's relationship to His people is in terms of a covenant. The focus here is on the covenant and Abraham's response

to the covenant promises. Study **15:1–18; 17:1–27;** and **18:1–15.** Note in each instance what is promised and Abraham's response to the promises. Does his reaction in each case denote faith or doubt?

Discuss how we react to God's promises of salvation and help. Do we believe or doubt? Why?

2. Evidence of the breakdown of the marriage relationship is found in **16:1–6.** What weaknesses of Abraham and Sarah contribute to their conflict? Is either one able to accept responsibility for the difficulty?

How does Sarah show signs of being related spiritually to Eve? Abraham to Adam?

How does God intervene in **16:7–15** to undo what the two have done?

3. Read over the events in **chapter 19.** What does the account say about the dangers of living among people who want only to practice their sin?

How can our own relationship to God be corrupted by evil friends or companions?

Is it possible to live or work among people who are openly sinful and scornful of God and not be affected?

How does the event in **19:26** serve as a special warning?

4. Read **chapter 20.** What elements of sin and weakness on the part of Abraham do you find?

What judgment of God is there?

What act of saving or promise?

Creation Now

1. Many are troubled by doubt. When life is good, God seems unnecessary; when life is bad, God seems distant. The reality of our scientific world and our complacent style of living seem to drive God out. God's repeated promises of forgiveness and salvation are very clear in Scripture, but some still struggle to believe and receive His grace. What is God's reaction to the obvious doubt of Abraham and Sarah? What does that say about the way we ought to deal with those suffering with doubt?

What specific things can you, as individuals and/or as a group, do to help people recognize, admit, and deal with their doubt?

How does the way Jesus deals with Thomas in **John 20:24–29** help?

How does the message of God's constant love and forgiveness relate to our doubt?

2. We have looked in some detail at God's covenant promise to Abraham and his descendants. If you had to write the "new covenant" God gave us through Christ, what would it be? Try to answer these questions as they relate to you personally:

a. What has God promised to you because of Jesus Christ?

b. What is the reason He has promised this to you?

c. What assurance, or seal, of the promise do you have from God that insures the promises?

d. What is expected of you?

e. How is this covenant different from the covenant God made with Abraham?

Lesson 6

And Now the Good News
(Genesis 21–23)

Introduction

What are you willing to give? The question comes up often in churches. How much will your faith in God impel you to return to Him? Five percent? Ten percent? The Internal Revenue Service thinks 10 percent is about right. And how much time will you give to Sunday school and bake sales, work days and collection drives, stewardship calls, and all of that? Can we give an hour a week—or more? two? three? four?

Abraham astounds us. So often he seems to muddle through life. He cannot seem to understand God's promises or believe them. He repeats the same mistakes. He can't seem to keep his own household together. And yet when God says, "Go," Abraham goes.

Now we see him with a knife poised above his own son, the son of his old age, the son whom he treasures. Abraham is willing to sacrifice his child at God's command. What unbelievable faith!

Could we even come close?

Overview

Several seemingly unimportant events surround the center of attention in this portion of **Genesis**. There are two encounters between Abraham and his neighbors that go into some detail establishing the claim of the people of Israel to the well at Beersheba (the well of the oath), **21:22–32,** and the grave plot of Sarah, **23:1–20.** The text deals with great care with the purchase of the grave in the land of the Hittites. It apparently means to fix Abraham's roots in the land and overcome any later question about the right of the people of Israel to the land.

But the real focus is again on Abraham and his own. Strife remains.

Sarah, even after the joyful gift of the child of her old age, cannot seem to overcome her jealousy of Hagar, and again Hagar is driven away. Again God rescues Hagar in the wilderness and, this time, establishes her and her son away from the tents of Abraham.

The focus narrows on the faith of Abraham. God kept His promise and gave Abraham the long-awaited child. **Chapter 22** shows us one of the most remarkable tests of faith ever given. Abraham is asked to sacrifice his own son.

How much do you love God, Abraham? How much are you willing to sacrifice at God's command? Will you give your son, Abraham?

Every parent must feel the torture in Abraham's soul as he makes his way to the place of the sacrifice. Every parent knows the fear and doubt and pain Abraham must have experienced.

Can anyone love so much that he would sacrifice his own son? Did God? Christ calls us to reflect such love toward the Father **(Matthew 10:37)**.

Focus 1: Roots

1. Read **Genesis 22** and **John 3:16**. What important root statement about God and the New Testament is in these two passages?

How does the account in **Genesis** give God's gift of His Son more meaning?

2. Read **23:1–20.** It was unthinkable for a patriarch to be buried in a place where he did not belong (see **47:27–31**). Why would the purchase of the grave be of particular importance to Abraham? to his descendants?

What does it say about the promises of God?

3. One of the repeated revelations of God in Scripture is that of protector or preserver, especially of the oppressed. Read **21:8–21** with that in mind. In this case, and in **chapter 16,** how does God demonstrate that He is protector of the oppressed?

Read **Isaiah 35:3–6** and **61:1.** How is the helper or protector role carried through to the Messiah?

In **Matthew 11:4–6,** how does Jesus assure John that He truly is the Messiah? In what way does Jesus reflect the role of helper in His life? What does that mean for us if we seek to imitate Him?

Focus 2: Relationships

1. Read **21:1–8.** What does the account say about the way God fulfills His covenant promises?

What is important about the fact that the son was a child of their old age?

Why the name *Isaac* ("he laughs")?

2. What is there in Abraham's character that makes his obedience in **chapter 22** so unlikely?

Review **12:10–13** and **20:11–13.** How do those events seem to indicate a weakness of character in Abraham?

How is it possible for him to overcome his weakness and to do willingly what God commands in **chapter 22?**

Read **Romans 7:14–20** and **8:32.** How do Paul's words expose the struggle we all have with our sinfulness as we seek to do God's will?

3. Reread **chapter 22,** but this time put yourself in Abraham's and Isaac's place. Pause after **verses 2, 3, 5, 7, 8, 10,** and **12** and talk about what Abraham and Isaac must have felt at that time. What does their ability to go on say about the strength of their faith?

What is it in each of the relationships—God to Abraham, Abraham to God, Abraham to Isaac, and Isaac to Abraham—that is particularly beautiful and important? What does each say about our relationships?

4. What does Abraham's covenant with Abimelech in **21:22–34** and his purchase of the cave in **23:3–16** tell us about his relationship to the other inhabitants of Canaan?

What might this suggest about our relationship to others who are not God's people?

Creation Now

The idea that God uses people who are apparently weak to complete magnificent acts of faith is often repeated in Scripture. You might review a few: Samson—**Judges 13–16;** Gideon—**Judges 6–7;** and Peter—

Matthew 26:69–75; Acts 4:1–13. We often think we are not qualified or able to do great things for God. What is it in us that God can use for His purposes?

Does His selection of people in Scripture indicate that He always chooses the most able or the best prepared to do His will?

Talk about some of the tasks God may have for you and how He gives you the strength to do them.

Lesson 7

A Chosen Family
(Genesis 24–26)

Introduction

One would think and hope that if Christian love is going to work anywhere, it would work in our homes. Families are committed to each other and love each other.

But it doesn't seem to work that way. A part of each home, Christian or not, is conflict—sometimes bitter strife and jealousy, oftentimes hurting others and being hurt. Why?

Our families are no more perfect than the people in them. The very closeness that enables us to show love also puts us close enough to cause pain.

The situation is not new. God's chosen—Isaac and his God-selected bride, Rebekah, and their God-given children—live in something less than harmony. There is jealousy, deceit, rancor, and even threats of revenge.

Things have not changed much since then.

Overview

These people are much like their parents and grandparents. They reflect the strengths and weaknesses of their ancestors. Isaac marries the wife of God's choosing without question **(24:67)**. He lives where he is told to live **(26:2–6)**. He goes out of his way to live at peace with his neighbors **(26:16–24)**. And yet the weaknesses are there too. He passes off his wife as his sister **(26:7–11)**, as had his father, and he does not deal with the bitterness and strife that develop in his own home.

Chapter 24 is a detailed account of the search for, and the finding of, a wife for Isaac. Abraham cannot allow Isaac to leave the Promised Land, nor can he permit him to corrupt the family by marrying a Canaanite. A wife must be found from the family. The wife, Rebekah, is chosen by God. Interestingly, neither Isaac nor Rebekah nor her family object to the marriage.

Abraham (25:1–5) gives everything to Isaac, but the wealth does not give Isaac a happy home. His twin sons, Esau and Jacob, begin a power struggle even before they are born. Their parents join the struggle, choosing one son over the other.

Jacob ("deceiver"), true to his name, manipulates his twin brother out of his birthright—an act in which Esau willingly participates. Jacob sets the stage for a later deception of his father.

But God is faithful to His promise and repeats it again to Isaac (26:1–4, 23–25). The covenant is demonstrated by God's action among His people.

Focus 1: Roots

1. Israel has always had a tradition of acrimony with her Canaanite neighbors. Even at the time of Christ there was hatred in the attitude of the Jews toward the Samaritans. Part of the reason for the strife was that the Israelites often self-righteously flaunted their election and looked down on their neighbors. The roots of this self-righteous attitude are partially in the misunderstanding of Abraham's action in seeking a wife who is not a Canaanite. Read 24:1–9; Deuteronomy 7:3–4; Joshua 23:12–13; and skim Ezra 9–10. What do you think was the reason for the careful avoidance of intermarriage with the Canaanites?

What kind of trouble for the people of Israel often resulted from intermarriage?

To what extent should we seek exclusiveness in our relationships with others, especially in marriage?

Read **1 Corinthians 7:10–18.** What might be some of the concerns of marrying an unbeliever? a person of another denomination?

2. Part of the tradition of the parental choosing of marriage partners comes from this account **(chapter 24).** The choosing was done to benefit the family and nation. Why is the system of parental arrangement of marriage almost unknown today? Would it work today?

If your parents had picked your spouse, would they have picked the person you married? Why or why not?

Do you think it is a good idea for you to help your children choose their spouses?

3. **Genesis 25:1–4** and **12–18** describe what happens to the other descendants of Abraham. They are definitely not "chosen." What reason is there for the strong identification of the "chosen" one in the family?

What roots for our New Testament faith are in this "choosing"?

4. Isaac evidences his roots in his father. Read **26:1–10** and **26:26–33**—compare to **12:10–20; 20:1–18;** and **21:22–32.** What repetition of his father's actions do you find in Isaac?

What strengths and weaknesses? How is he like his father?

Focus 2: Relationships

1. Abraham's servant allows God to choose Rebekah **(24:10–52).** In what sense does God choose our mate for us?

What things might be good to look for in someone before marriage?

2. Jacob's relationship to his brother is not harmonious from the first. Read **25:27–28.** How do the parents contribute to the difficulty?

Is it ever right to favor one child over another? On the other hand, is it possible to feel exactly the same about each child?

What is the best way to handle our mixed feelings about our children?

3. Of what importance is it that God directly acts in Rebekah's pregnancy (**25:21**)? In what sense are these children of promise?

Read also **26:23–25**. How is the promise like that given to Abraham?

In what way is the gift of the children and its resulting promise of "greatness" tied to the promise of the Savior?

Creation Now

Sometimes we think that a Christian home is filled with sweetness and light and people who are always kind, courteous, and loving. The view of

Isaac's family, the family of the chosen one, is hardly perfect. How can it damage members of a family if they expect others to be perfect and are then disappointed in themselves and others when they are not?

Read **Colossians 3:12–17** and **Ephesians 5:21–6:4.** Then talk about these questions or others you may suggest: What makes a home a Christian home?

What does forgiveness have to do with making a home truly Christian? What is the best way to handle our difficulties and our differences?

In what way can we make our conflicts more constructive?

How is it possible for conflict to lead to healing instead of pain?

Lesson 8

It's Not My Fault
(Genesis 27–28)

Introduction

Your husband (wife) brings you a gift. There is no special occasion—the gift just says, "I love you." The gift turns out to be awful—an ugly piece of clothing. Now what? Do you tell the truth? What about hurting the giver's feelings? Or do you tell an untruth? Do you say (with feeling) that you "simply love it"? Are we required to tell the truth in this situation? Which is worse, the untruth or the hurt?

Some would have us believe that a loving reason makes anything right. They would tell us that it is not the act itself that determines "rightness" or "wrongness" but the intention of the act. Therefore, to tell an untruth, to take something from a neighbor, or to experiment sexually is all right, if done for a loving reason.

Is that right? Are we permitted to break a rule for the "right" reason? Does the purpose of an act determine its rightness?

Was it all right for Rebekah and Jacob to fool Isaac if it was for a good reason?

Does the end ever justify the means?

Overview

This section of **Genesis** is like a play. There is plot, dialog, conflict, and suspense. You can see these elements played out as you read the chapters.

Picture old Isaac. He has done his best to raise his family. Even though he always favored Esau, he has tried to be fair. He is blind now and facing death. Sadly, he cannot trust his own family.

Look at Rebekah. As a young woman, she seemed so loving and kind. What has changed her into a scheming deceiver? Could it be the terrible way she is treated by Esau's wives? Or has her communication with Isaac stopped altogether? Rebekah is no fool. She knows how to get what she wants. And she wants that blessing for her son Jacob.

What kind of child is Jacob? Obedient to his mother to the letter of what she tells him, yet deceitful enough to cheat his brother and lie to his father. Somehow he is religious as well. He sees a vision and is so awed by the presence of God in that place that he makes a vow to God and sets that place aside for worship.

Then there is Esau. How could this wild child come from these gentle people? Is it possible that he is more like his mother than his father? He laments his own foolishness for selling his birthright, and he determines to avenge himself by killing his brother. This account is almost like Cain and Abel revisited.

Like their ancestors before them, the little family lives out the result of their sin. The account says something about them, but it says even more about their roots in the past and their need for a Savior.

Focus 1: Roots

Do a character study of the four main characters: Isaac, Rebekah, Jacob, and Esau. Answer these questions: What strengths and weaknesses do you find in each person?

In what way do they show their relationship to Adam and Eve?

In what way do they show their relationship to God?

In what way is this person like you?

What can you see in the person to help you look at your own roots and relationships?
Use these passages or others you might find:
Isaac: **22:10; 24:66–67; 25:28; 26:6–9, 16–17.**
Rebekah: **24:15–21, 58; 25:28; 27:5–17, 42–46.**
Jacob: **25:26, 28–33; 27:14–29, 36; 28:7, 11–22.**
Esau: **25:27, 34; 27:41; 28:6–9.**

Focus 2: Relationships

1. Read **chapter 27** again. Look for breakdowns in relationships. What evidence can you find to conclude that the marriage relationship and the relationship of parents to children and brother to brother had broken down in Isaac's home? To what would you attribute that breakdown?

How can Isaac's family be a warning to us?

2. Who was at fault in the deceit? Rebekah or Jacob? Rebekah planned the whole thing (27:5–17). Is she responsible? Jacob willingly went along (27:18–27). Is Jacob at fault?

Are we responsible to obey our parents and others in authority when they tell us to do something wrong?

What about the government? What about a boss?

3. Read 27:30–41. Can you understand Esau's feelings? Was he justified in trying to get back at Jacob?

Why is it particularly hard to forgive people who are very close to us when they hurt us?

What does Jesus say about the way we are to deal with our "brother" (**Matthew 18:21–22**)?

Is forgiveness ever easy? Was God's forgiveness easy? Why or why not?

4. Read **28:13–15.** God repeats the promise now to Jacob. Why does God not reject Jacob and his deceitful ways?

What does that say about God's promises to His people?

5. Read **28:18–22.** Is it a good idea to make this kind of a promise to God? Is it required?

Was Jacob putting God to the test? What might be the benefit of making this kind of a promise to God?

Creation Now

1. Are we ever put into situations where a choice must be made but both alternatives seem wrong? How about the example in the Introduction? Other situations might be as follows: (a) You are asked by a friend's husband not to tell your friend that she is terminally ill, and she asks you about her condition. (b) A couple calls and wants to come over to visit. You really don't feel like socializing, but you don't want to hurt their feelings. (c) You must decide whether to use artificial means to prolong the life of a loved one, even though recovery is hopeless, or "turn off the machines" and hasten death. Perhaps you can think of other situations. What should be the basis for our choices in those cases?

Are we to try to justify what we have chosen? Is it possible to declare any action correct because of the "intention" of the act?

What do the Scriptures say about this? What does the death and resurrection of Jesus have to say to us in these situations?

2. Does the end ever justify the means? Does the fact that Rebekah was taking care of her son and doing what she considered to be the will of God justify what she did?

Did the fact that Jacob felt that he had a rightful claim to Esau's blessing (he bought it) justify the fact that he had to lie to get it?

Can we do things that are "slightly" illegal if it is for a good cause?

Is it all right to run bingo games or a raffle in places where those things are illegal in order to raise money for a "good cause"?

Matthew 10:16 and **Luke 16:1–11** seem to indicate that we are to be as crafty as the people of the world. Does this apply to breaking the law, if it is for a good cause?

3. What reflections about Isaac's family do you find helpful for your own family?

What things do you see there that might cause you to repent and to seek God's help to do better?

Some consider family devotions to be a nice custom for the sake of the children, but why is it important that the members of a family talk and listen to one another in an atmosphere of trust?

Why is it necessary to go as a family to the cross of Christ?

Lesson 9

The Deceiver Is Deceived (Genesis 29–31)

Introduction

It's a "dog eat dog" world. Anyone in business will tell you that. It is almost impossible to be honest and still get ahead. Everyone expects kick-backs, payoffs, favors, special deals, or discounts. It's the way things work.

It's not exactly illegal—just kind of unfair. But who said life would be fair? You have to do your best and look out for yourself, don't you?

Jacob knew that. He was a good businessman. He knew how to make things work for him. He got what he wanted. How odd that he was not happy!

Overview

Jacob had it made—he was home free. He had arrived at his uncle's house with nothing and left with flocks, wives, children, and wealth. He had done it himself. He presented himself as a long-lost relative (29:1–14); worked for and earned two wives (29:15–30); gained 11 sons through his wives and their slave girls (29:31–20:24); made a shrewd deal with Laban that resulted in ownership of a large part of Laban's flocks (30:25–43); and he escaped before he could be called to account for his misdeeds (31:1–21). He had everything going his way. Even God continued to promise to bless him.

And yet he was not a happy man. Whom could Jacob trust? He could not trust his family. They had been cheating each other for years. His brother was out to kill him. He could not trust his uncle. Jacob and Laban had been in a power struggle for 20 years. He could not trust his cousins. They thought he had been stealing from their father. He could not trust his wives. They had their own power struggle going. And he could not even trust his "beloved"—she risked his neck and aggravated her father by stealing some household idols. Perhaps, in the end, he could not even trust himself. Maybe he was so frightened of his uncle and his brother because he was not at peace with himself or with God.

Jacob seemed to have it made, still he was afraid. At least he did have God to turn to when all else failed. God was still there. His promises remained. All the success of the world is finally disappointing if one is apart from God.

Focus 1: Roots

1. What evidence of a strong faith do you see in Jacob and Laban in **31:45–55?**

How is their agreement different from the covenant between God and man?

2. What roots of idolatry and superstition do you see in **30:27; 31:19;** and **31:30–35?**

In what way do we sometimes fall victim to "little" superstitions (horoscopes, good luck charms, etc.)? Are these wrong?

Read **Deuteronomy 18:9–13.** Are they dangerous? In what way?

3. The roots of the nation of Israel and the coming Savior are here. Read **29:30–30:24.** These men, together with Benjamin, who was born later, became the fathers of the 12 tribes of Israel. Add their names to the Genesis Family Tree at the end of this book. Which of these sons became the most important? Which is important in tracing the birth of the Savior?

Focus 2: Relationships

The account in **chapters 29–31** reads easily. It is interesting, almost fascinating, to see Jacob do his thing and get what he wants. But it takes on a frightening note when we realize that these are relatives gouging each other for money, possessions, and power.

1. After reading the account, study **29:25; 30:31–33; 30:34–36; 30:37–42,** and the meeting between Jacob and Laban in **31:20–44.** If you were a judge and had to decide between these two men as to who was the "injured" party and who had a just claim to the flocks and property, what would you decide? Give reasons for your answer.

How does this conflict demonstrate the sinfulness of these people and their relationship to Adam and Eve?

What advice might you have for them personally?

2. The chapters are full of complaining. Read **30:1; 30:15; 31:1–2; 31:14–15; 31:26;** and **31:36–41.** What were some of the basic causes of the complaining?

When you hear members of your own family complaining, what are they really trying to say?

What is the best way to handle complaining?

3. Sin leads us to a good view of others' faults and a blindness to our own. How does the encounter between Jacob and Laban illustrate this truth?

What does Jesus say in **Matthew 7:1–5** about our ability to find fault?

What does the cross say to us about fault finding?

4. Again, God becomes the protector of the oppressed. Read **29:31.** What does this say about God's attitude toward those who are misused or hurt?

How does the life of Jesus illustrate this truth about God?

Creation Now

1. Jacob and Laban seemed to do what was necessary in order to get ahead, even if it meant deceiving and misusing one another. Today, is it possible to be successful in business and still be completely honest? Can a person of integrity make it in our world?

What makes it difficult to be honest?

What help can we in the church give to those who struggle with this problem?

2. What might have happened to Jacob if he had taken Jesus' advice and "turned the other cheek" when he was cheated and deceived by his uncle? Would he have lost out?

Is it true that the people of the world will take advantage of a person who tries to be honest and giving?

What help do we have from the life of Christ and from His death and resurrection that might make it possible for us to be more giving in a taking world?

3. The account of the relationship between Jacob and his two wives is very sad. Leah is unloved. What must her life have been like? How did it make her bitter and vengeful?

What is the most important gift we can give to our spouse and children? What might be the cost if we do not?

Lesson 10

Jacob Wrestles (Genesis 32–36)

Introduction

What if you or I had been by the brook when the angel of the Lord came to wrestle **(32:22–30)**? What would we have done?

Would we have passively accepted as the "will of God" whatever the angel would do to us? Or, having recognized the angel, would we have tried to flee?

Isn't that what we usually do with "messengers" (trials—**James 1:2**) of God—with those difficult things that come upon us and try our faith and trust in Him? We lie down. We plead for help. We say, "Please, Lord, do it for me. Take it away for me."

Jacob did not. He wrestled. He held on. Even when he was hurt, he insisted that the angel bless him.

Have you ever wrestled with God or with His messenger? Have you demanded a blessing out of a situation that seemed hopeless, painful, or impossible? Have you ever wrestled and won?

Jacob did. Even Jacob, the deceiver. He was given the name *Israel*. What is the significance of this new name?

Overview

Of all of the accounts of the life of Jacob, **chapters 32–33** are the most flattering. Here Jacob is shown not as a crafty manipulator, but as a loving brother returning home **(32:1–21)**, as a provider and protector of his family **(33:1–3)**, as a valiant warrior in a mysterious struggle with a messenger of God **(32:22–30),** and as an eager, generous gift-giver when he finally meets Esau **(33:8–11)**.

Surely the trouble is still there. **Chapter 34** makes it clear that all things are not going well for Jacob, either with his children (two of his sons violate an agreement and kill all the men of a village and plunder it) or with his neighbors. After the plundering, Jacob and his sons are treated with some mistrust by the people in the area.

But Jacob shows his religious dedication to the Lord in **chapter 35**. He builds an altar to God at Bethel and makes an effort to do away with all of the false gods and superstitions in his family. And God blesses him **(35:9)**.

Several other events occur that must have caused Jacob great pain. His eldest son betrays him and has sexual relations with one of his concubines **(35:22)**. Jacob's beloved Rachel dies **(35:16–20)**, and his father dies **(35:27–29)**.

In these chapters, as in others, Jacob shows strength and weakness, faith and doubt. He has joy and sorrow. He is God's chosen, and God still loves him.

Focus: Roots and Relationships

Throughout this portion of **Genesis** we see Jacob in the process of struggle. He is struggling not so much against others as with himself. A great part of our life, like Jacob's, is spent working through internal conflict. Let's look at him and see what we can learn about the roots of our own inner battles, and how relationships to others and to God are involved in our conflicts.

1. Jacob encounters fear **(32:7)**. He was afraid for himself and others. He does a number of things about it. His immediate response is to prepare for the worst **(32:8)**. Then he does what many people do when they are in a difficult situation **(32:9–12)**. He acts and tries to soften the threat **(32:13–21)**. Jacob seems to overcome his fear as he enters a battle with an angel of God and wins **(32:22–32)**.

What is our usual reaction when we are afraid? How do we learn to handle our fear?

How much of fear is related to our relationships to other people? to our own inner weakness?

Is it possible to overcome fear?

What does Jacob do that might guide us when dealing with fear?

What is the most powerful weapon we have in the struggle with fear? What promise does God give in **1 John 4:18** concerning fear?

What are some of the things we can do to help one another deal with our fears?

2. Jacob encounters joy and pain in reunion and separation. Read **33:3–5; 35:16–21;** and **35:27–29.** What kinds of feelings must these events have had for Jacob?

Are joy and grief related? In what way, for you?

Why does there often seem to be a little sadness, even in the greatest joy?

In what sense does the Christian have joy, even in the midst of the terrible sadness caused by the death of a loved one?

What does **Romans 12:15** indicate is our Christian response to those who are rejoicing or weeping?

In what way can we help ourselves and others to enjoy fully the happy times and to soften the pain of the times of sadness?

3. Jacob encountered disappointment in his loved ones. Read **34:25–31** and **35:22.** What kinds of feelings would Jacob have had at these events? What kind of pain might he have felt?

One of the risks of loving is the possibility that those we love will disappoint us and hurt us. Read **Matthew 23:37** and **Luke 19:41–44.** How does Jesus express His extreme disappointment? What is His attitude toward those who have disappointed Him?

What is to be our attitude toward those we love who cause us pain by letting us down?

Is there ever to be a limit to our love? Does God set a limit on His love when we disappoint Him?

4. Jacob encounters God in prayer and worship. Read **32:9–12** and **35:1–15.** In one case Jacob prays as a response to a fearful situation. In the other, he worships as an act of faith in response to the instruction and blessing of God. Which worship is easier?

Why is it difficult, sometimes, to come to God when things are going well for us?

In what way may difficult experiences be used by God for our good?

What is the purpose of worship?

Creation Now

Jacob is tested by the encounter with the "man" **(32:22–32). Deuteronomy 8:2** and **James 1:2** indicate that God sends trials and hardships to test His people. These trials can be various kinds of hardships that test our faith. Jacob does the difficult thing—he wrestles. In what sense are we to "wrestle" with God when something difficult comes into our lives?

If we are caught in sickness, sorrow, or a painful situation, are we simply to accept it as the will of God and make the best of it?

What do Jesus' compliments for the Syrophoenician woman **(Matthew 15:21–28)** and the centurion **(Matthew 8:5–10)** say about the necessity that our faith "contend" with God?

What promises of God do we have that equip us to "contend" with Him?

How is it possible that even in a difficult or painful situation our contending with God and seeking His help to overcome will make us stronger in the future?

Does God promise to help us in all our encounters with His messengers? How can we help each other to deal with difficult situations and to grow in faith by those encounters?

Lesson 11

Meet a Hero
(Genesis 37–41)

Introduction

John said, "Do not be surprised, my brothers, if the world hates you" **(1 John 3:13).**

Surprised? We would be astounded. The world hardly notices us.

Sure we are Christians, but we don't have to wear it on our sleeves, do we? After all, we can't go around singing psalms and saying prayers and preaching on every street corner. People would think we're crazy. Besides, faith is a private matter, isn't it?

Joseph was a man of faith. He was selected by God and set apart as someone special. His brothers hated him and sold him into slavery.

Daniel was a man of faith. He was selected by God as someone special, and he practiced his faith with commitment. Some hated him and threw him into a lions' den.

Jeremiah was chosen. He refused to participate in the evil life around him. He spoke judgment on the foolishness of the people of his day. The king's officials hated him and threw him into a well.

Jesus was chosen. He was the Messiah. He spoke the truth about who He was and what His mission was. Many people hated Him too. They nailed Him to a cross.

We are chosen—"called out," "holy." Isn't it odd that the world often doesn't notice us? Much of the time no one would suspect that we are Christians.

Overview

Now in our long trek through **Genesis** we come to a truly good man. Here is someone to admire. Joseph is apparently faithful and honest.

Of course he had minor problems. He seems somewhat arrogant, and he delights in "telling" on his brothers **(37:2)**.

The deeds of Joseph are Sunday school favorites. He is favored by God and his father, and both give him gifts **(37:3; 39:2)**. He is sold into slavery **(37:12–28)** and immediately rises to a position of responsibility and power **(39:1–6)**. Even after he is thrown into prison for something he did not do, he is given special responsibilities **(39:19–23)**. And when he impresses the Pharaoh with his insight into dreams (a gift from God), he is put in charge of the whole land of Egypt **(chapter 41)**.

But what is interesting is the response of the people around Joseph. His brothers hate him **(37:4)**. His father is offended by him **(37:10)**. After he is made head of Potiphar's house, he offends his master's wife by his rejection of her, and she furiously turns on him **(39:7–18)**. His presence seems to be an accusation to many of those around him.

It was much the same with Jesus! Many of the responses of the religious leaders seemed to be reactions to the accusing presence of Jesus Himself. His life seems to say, "This is what you would act like if you were true religious leaders."

And Joseph seems to say by his goodness, "This is what you would be like if you were a child of God." Neither of them was well received.

Focus 1: Roots

1. **Chapter 38** is omitted in the Introduction and Overview. It is about Judah and his son Perez, who became a part of the lineage of Jesus. What would you say might be the message of the chapter? What does it say about Jesus?

2. Dreams are important here. Some of the revelation of the will of God in Scripture comes by dreams **(Matthew 1:20–21; 2:12–13)**. Do you think God reveals His will in dreams today? Do they foretell the future?

What caution might you express to those who put their faith in dreams?

3. Joseph is as close as the book of **Genesis** comes to a real hero in the sense that we use the word. In what way was he a hero?

Would he be noticed as different in our day? What is it that made him different from the others?

Are we to strive to be like Joseph?

What comparisons can you find between Joseph and Jesus?

Focus 2: Relationships

1. Often one child in a family is exceptionally bright or good-looking or talented. What was Jacob's response to his "favored" child **(37:3)**? What about Joseph's brothers **(37:4)**?

What about Joseph's own response as he tells his brothers the dream (37:5–7, 9–10)?

What should the attitude of a person who is unusually talented or gifted be toward those who are less able? Should they be proud? Why or why not?

How should parents relate to such a gifted child? How can they affirm the goodness and the gifts of the special child without hurting the other children?

Was there anything Jacob could have done to avert the incident in 37:21–24?

2. Read 34:31–35. How does the event illustrate the truth that one wrong action often leads to another?

Is it true that when we intend to hurt someone, we often end up hurting someone else?

How must the brothers have felt when they saw their father's grief? Do you think they repented?

What should we do when we feel remorse over having hurt someone?

How can we be sure we are forgiven also by God?

3. Read **chapters 39–41.** In all of these events Joseph acts with integrity, kindness, and honesty. In **chapter 39** his reward is unjust punishment **(39:19–20).** In **chapter 40** his service to the two in prison is ignored **(40:23).** When he interprets the Pharaoh's dream, he is rewarded by being given a place of power and importance **(41:37–46).** Which response to acts of kindness and honesty do you think is most common?

Is it true that we can expect to suffer when we attempt to do the will of God in our lives? when we speak the Gospel to people?

Is it normal for people to repay us for kindness? How did they respond to Jesus' kindness?

Creation Now

Jesus said, "By this all men will know that you are My disciples, if you love one another" **(John 13:35).** Is it possible for people outside of the church and those who see our homes to tell that we are believers by the way we act?

If we truly live our faith, will we not provoke both hostility and admiration as Joseph did?

What is the purpose of "doing good"? Why is it easier to blend in with the crowd?

In what sense are we to be in the world—yet "holy," set apart, as Joseph and Jesus were?

On the other hand, is it possible to drive people away from God by our goodness? In what way?

How did Paul outline his relationship to the people around him in **1 Corinthians 9:19–23?** Is that to be our model?

What events in Jesus' life guide our relationship to others?

What about His words in **John 15:17–19?**

What should be the direction and purpose of our relationships to the people outside the family of God?

Lesson 12

A Change for the Better
(Genesis 42–47)

Introduction

Sometimes the past is an incredible weight. It may be one mistake or a repeated sin that shrouds our life or haunts us like a demon. We cannot seem to forget it or overcome it.

We hear the words of forgiveness. They tell us over and over that God forgives. We come again to the cross of Christ and hear the message of forgiveness. We celebrate Christ's glorious resurrection.

But still the pain of guilt does not leave us. It drives us into ourselves and separates us from God. It interferes with our relationships to others.

Joseph's brothers knew the reality of guilt. Their act against Joseph, whether done out of youthful irresponsibility or in jealous anger of the moment, was never far from their thoughts. As they saw their father age and get closer to death, they must have longed to rid themselves of the guilt by telling him, but they could not.

And so they went on with their burden of guilt. They needed a Savior too.

Overview

Throughout this portion of **Genesis,** Joseph continues as a hero. Often his acts seem confused by his mixed feelings: joy at seeing his brothers again; caution that they might still be as hostile as they had been; the temptation to use his power to get revenge. Still he acts with kindness and concern for them and for his father.

But how much his brothers have changed! Those wild, careless young men, who tried to destroy a brother and almost killed their father with grief, are older and wiser now. They are obedient **(42:1–3),** courteous **(42:10–13; 43:28),** repentant **(42:20–22),** and self-sacrificing **(42:37; 43:8–9).** They genuinely seem to care about their father and do not wish to cause him further pain **(44:34)**. Most important, they no longer hate their father's favorite (Benjamin), but they protect him **(44:18–22)**. Joseph forgives his brothers **(45:5)**.

Jacob still laments the death of Joseph **(42:36),** and he fears so much for Benjamin that he will not let him go with the others to Egypt. But he is finally rewarded with happiness at being reunited with Joseph **(46:28–30)** and prepares for the end of his life in Egypt, having been promised by God that he and his descendants will someday return to the Promised Land **(46:1–4)**.

The whole account reads like a heartwarming drama. The human emotions are there—sorrow and joy, fear and frustration, need and giving, kindness and care. There is love—love shown by a man for his children and by the children for their father and for each other. Under it all, the guiding hand of God is there, caring for His own.

Focus 1: Roots

1. Read **46:1–4.** What roots of the exodus do you find in these verses?

Did the people of Israel ever consider Egypt their home?

Why was it so important to them to return to their own land?

How does God show His personal concern for Jacob in this promise?

2. Read **42:37** and **43:8–10.** What is remarkable about those statements?

What do they say about how the two brothers had changed?

In this case, how does their action point to Christ?

How are their actions different from Christ's self-sacrifice?

Focus 2: Relationships

1. Joseph met his brothers several times **(chapters 42, 43,** and **44)** before he was willing to reveal himself to them, even though his emotions almost overcame him. Why do you think he delayed?

Why did he put the cup into Benjamin's sack **(44:1–10)?**

What was it that finally assured him that it was all right to reveal himself to his brothers (44:18–34)?

In what ways do we test people to see if we can trust them with our feelings?

Why is this testing necessary?

What gifts do we have in Christ that can help us overcome some of the need to test one another?

2. Jacob's relationship to his sons is still not perfect. He seems to hold them responsible for his trouble. Read 42:1; 42:36; and 43:6. What accusing words are there?

How must Jacob's sons have felt?

Jacob had changed too. He seems resigned to his fate **(43:11)**. How is that a different attitude than when he was younger?

What weaknesses, common to all of us, do you see here in Jacob?

3. Read **45:25–28** and **46:28–30.** Can you describe the feelings of the two men?

Can you remember times of great joy that you have experienced? Did they involve other people?

How did those experiences affect your relationship to God?

What promise of reunion do we have that others, without Christ, do not have?

How can we sense some of the joy of heaven in experiences like Jacob's and Joseph's?

Creation Now

Through most of their life the brothers of Joseph must have suffered terrible guilt. They had committed a real crime. They had almost destroyed their father by killing (they thought) their brother. **Genesis 42:20–23** indicates that the guilt was not far from their minds, and **42:35–38** indicates that Jacob was not above calling it to their attention.

How do you think the guilt affected their life and their relationships to their father? to the other brothers? to their own families? to God?

Why is guilt so devastating? How does it make us feel about ourselves?

In the case of the brothers, it was real guilt for a real act that they were suffering. How does the message of Christ's death and resurrection free us from that kind of guilt?

How can our experiences of forgiveness be as freeing as Joseph's forgiveness was for his brothers?

Sometimes we suffer with false guilt. It is imagined or exaggerated guilt—the kind of guilt that makes us feel worthless and empty. How can we deal with that kind of guilt?

What can we do for each other to help work out that feeling of worthlessness?

How can the message of forgiveness help us?

Lesson 13

An End That Is a Beginning (Genesis 47:29–50:26)

Introduction

We have struggled with Jacob through his life. We have seen him grow from a crafty young man to a caring father. We have seen his fortune grow from nothing to great wealth and power. And yet he dies.

Even our hero dies. Joseph, who worked his way up from prison to power, who showed the brilliance of mind and tenderness of heart that made both survival and success come to his family and his father's family, also dies.

Is that the way it always ends? Is that the story of life?

Genesis is only the beginning. By its name and nature it leads into the rest of the revelation of God. It cries to us: "Look! This is not the end. It is just the beginning of the loving, choosing, forgiving, and saving acts of God among His people."

The message of Jesus on the cross is also a message of beginning. Out of the death of Good Friday comes new life on the Easter day of resurrection. Out of the death of two elderly men in this portion of **Genesis** comes new life and promise. And God's hand acts to save.

God still controls. Even to the end of our own life, which is really no end at all. It is the beginning of eternal life in heaven.

Overview

There is great sadness in this portion of **Genesis**. It deals with preparation for death, death itself, and burial. It seems to be an ending.

Jacob's relationship to his sons comes to an end, not just in death, but in a kind of prophetic revelation of their future as part of the new nation called by Jacob's new name (Israel—**49:1–28**).

Jacob's relation to his favorite son ends. He blesses Joseph's sons and takes them as his own (48:1–22).

Jacob's life ends. He is given a solemn promise that he will be buried in Canaan (47:27–31) and is embalmed and buried in the grave of his choosing. His death is a very sad event, and Joseph deeply mourns his father (49:29–50:14).

Joseph also dies. The final words of the book are the account of his death and burial (50:22–26).

The whole section, even though it is an end, gives marks of new beginnings. Jacob's words of promise to his sons speak of hope to them, which God will not fail to carry out. Facing the end of life, neither Joseph nor Jacob loses faith in the promises of God (50:24–25; 48:21–22).

The book ends as it began—with God acting to carry out His eternal purposes for His chosen people.

Focus 1: Roots—New Beginnings

1. What roots for the nation of Israel do you see in **chapters 48–49?**

Read **Joshua 13:1–7.** How did the action of Jacob in this portion of **Genesis** become the very foundation of the nation of Israel?

2. Read **50:22–26.** What roots of the exodus are here?

Amid the sadness of his own coming death, Joseph speaks words of sure confidence in the promises of God. What promise of God do we have in Christ that makes us confident also when we face our own death?

Is God's promise to us as sure as His promise to Joseph?

In what way does God continue to "save" His people of promise?

3. The roots of the Messiah are here. Read Jacob's promise to Judah in **49:8–10.** What king is told of as coming from Judah?

In what way does that promise point to Jesus?

Did God also keep that promise?

Focus 2: Relationships

1. Though the tradition of the people of that day was that the inheritance and the blessing should go to the oldest son, what theme is constantly repeated in **Genesis (48:13–15; 25:5; 27:1–29; 49:8–12)**?

In each case which son was "blessed"? What does that say about the hand of God as He is involved in choosing?

Why is it important for us to know that He is involved?

2. Two solemn human vows recorded in **Genesis** are in **24:3, 7** and **47:27–31.** What do they deal with? Why was this such an important concern for Abraham and for Jacob?

What is the land God promises us **(Revelation 21)?**

What does the longing of the patriarchs for their home say about our relationship to God and to heaven as our home?

3. Human relationships do not always end perfectly. How are Jacob's words to some of his sons rather harsh **(49:3–7)?**

Were these "promises" too harsh? How did they speak judgment?

Contrast the words with the way Joseph deals with his brothers in **50:15–21.** Which way of dealing with past hurts do you think is more like the way Christ deals with us?

Again, what do the exchanges say about God's attitude toward sin and His attitude toward the sinner?

Creation Now

The book of **Genesis** ends as human life ends—in death. No matter how hard we try to ignore or deny it, the truth is we all face death. It is part of our heritage from Adam and Eve.

Throughout the book of **Genesis,** death is not treated lightly. It is the curse of sin, and the death of a loved one causes deep sadness **(50:1).** What is the real cause of the pain at the death of someone close to us?

Does the fact that we hope for a resurrection free us from the pain of death?

Is it wrong to grieve over a death?

Read **1 Corinthians 15:51–58.** How do these words speak to our grief when someone we love dies?

How is it possible to come out of a time of grief with new hope?

What roots of that hope are here in **Genesis?**

Talk about ways in which that hope of eternal life with God through Christ can be shared with other people, especially with those who grieve. What does **Romans 12:15** say we are to do for those who grieve?

When is the right time to share the good news that God has promised new life in Christ, even in the face of death?

GENESIS
Rooted in Relationship

Leaders Notes

Leaders Notes

Preparing to Teach Genesis

In preparation to teach, consult introductions to the book of Genesis (e.g., The Concordia Self-Study Bible, *The Concordia Self-Study Commentary*) and if possible read the volume *Genesis* from *The People's Bible Commentary*.

Read the text in a modern translation. The NIV is referred to in the lesson comments.

Group Bible Study

Group Bible study means mutual learning from one another under the guidance of a leader or facilitator. The Bible is an inexhaustible resource. No one person can discover all it has to offer. In a class many eyes see many things and can apply them to many life situations. The leader should resist the temptation to "give the answers" or act as an "authority." This teaching approach can stifle participation by individual members and can actually hamper learning. As a general rule the teacher is not to "give interpretation" but to "develop interpreters." Of course, there are times when the leader should and must share insights and information gained by his or her own deeper research. The ideal class is one in which the leader guides class members through the lesson and engages them in meaningful discussion at all points, leading them to a summary of the lesson at the close. As a general rule, good leaders don't explain what the learners can discover by themselves.

Have a chalkboard and chalk or newsprint and markers available to record significant points of the lesson. Put your inquiries or the inquiries of participants into questions, problems, or issues. This provokes thought. Keep discussion to the point. List on the chalkboard or newsprint the answers given. Then determine the most vital points made in the discussion. Ask additional questions to fill apparent gaps.

The aim of every Bible study is to help people grow spiritually, not merely in biblical and theological knowledge, but in Christian thinking and living. This means growth in Christian attitudes, insights, and skills for

Christian living. The focus of this course must be the church and the world of our day. The guiding question will be, "What does the Lord teach us for life today?"

Teaching the Old Testament

Teaching an Old Testament book can become just ancient history if it is not applied to life in our times. Also, it can degenerate into moralizing, in which do-goodism becomes a substitute for the Gospel and sanctification gets confused with justification. The justified sinner is not moved by Law but by God's grace to a new life. A Christian's faith is always at work for Christ in every context of life. Meaningful, personal Christianity includes a loving trust in God that is evidenced in love for one's fellow human beings. Having experienced God's free grace and forgiveness, the Christian daily works in the world to reflect the will of God for humankind in every area of human endeavor.

The Christian leader is Gospel-oriented, not Law-oriented. He or she distinguishes Law from Gospel. Both are needed. There is no clear Gospel unless we first have been crushed by the Law and see our sinfulness. There is no genuine Christianity where faith is not followed by a life pleasing to God. In fact, genuine faith is inseparable from life. The Gospel alone gives us the new heart that causes us to love God and our neighbor.

When Christians teach the Old Testament, they do not teach it as a "law book" but instead as books containing both Law and Gospel. They see the God of the Old Testament as a God of grace, who out of love established a covenant of mercy with His people **(Deut. 7:6–10)** and forgave their sins. They interpret the Old Testament using the New Testament message in the fulfilled prophecy through Jesus Christ. They teach as leaders who personally know the Lord Jesus Christ as Savior, the victorious Christ who gives all believers a new life **(2 Cor. 5:17)** and a new mission **(John 20:21)**.

Pace Your Teaching

Do not try to cover every question in each lesson. This will lead to undue haste and frustration. Be selective. Pace your teaching. Spend no more than five minutes on the Introduction and two or three minutes on the Overview. Take time to go into the text paragraph by paragraph, but not verse by verse or word by word. Get the sweep of meaning. Occasionally stop to help the class gain understanding of a word or concept.

Do not allow any lesson to "drag" and become tiresome. Keep it moving. Keep it alive. Keep it meaningful. Eliminate some questions and restrict yourself to those questions most meaningful to your class.

Introduction

What is the meaning of all the events and complex genealogies of **Genesis?** They speak to us of our roots in God and our relationships to one another. You are encouraged to keep class discussion alive by centering on these roots and relationships. On completion of the class, the participants should have a clearer picture of what it means to be a creature of God, to be sinful from birth, and to be given life and salvation in Jesus Christ. If that is accomplished, the study of **Genesis** will have been valuable.

The course is divided into two parts. The first part deals with the early beginnings of humankind's history; the second part centers on the patriarchs—Abraham, Isaac, Jacob, and Joseph.

In each part, ask: What does this story say about God and His relationship to humankind and to me? What does this account say about my relationship to God and my roots in Him? And what does God want for me? How does this revelation expose my need for my Savior, Jesus Christ?

Note on the Name of God

The book of **Genesis** uses a number of names for God in the Hebrew (*Yahweh, El, Elohim,* and others). For the purposes of this study we will simply use the name *God* when referring to the Creator—occasionally using the personal name *Yahweh* (I Am) when it is needed for clarity.

Lesson 1

In the Beginning (Genesis 1–2)

Preparation for This Lesson

1. Read **Genesis 1–2.** As you read, think about what the chapters say about our roots and relationships.

2. Read a Bible commentary on the chapters. (Your pastor may be able to lend you one, or he can recommend one to borrow from the church library.)

3. Study the lesson material in the Study Guide and in this Guide. Choose those portions of the lesson that seem to be most meaningful for your class. Make additional notes and write questions that may occur to you.

4. One of the activities we will carry through this study is construction

of the "Family Tree" of man as outlined in **Genesis** and as it points to the coming Savior. Check the tree at the back of this book. You may want to make a larger copy of the tree on a sheet of poster board, with the names omitted so that they can be added as the class progresses.

5. Begin and end each session with worship. You may design your own worship or use the suggestions in this Guide.

Before the Session Begins

You will want to build relationships in your group. The Spirit works through our study of the Word to re-create us and to re-create our relationships with God and our fellow believers. You might lay the groundwork for that kind of growth by using some of your time in the first class period to begin the process of building relationships. Here are some suggestions:

1. Give each person time to present a little sketch of his or her life and background.

2. Form pairs and let them share something about themselves. Then ask the partner to present to the class the person with whom he or she has been speaking.

3. Let volunteers share one frustration and one joyful time they have recently experienced.

4. In order to get at the roots idea, talk about the national or ethnic origin of those in the class. Last names are a clue. Let them share something about their roots.

In each of these emphasize open and honest sharing. Each person in the class is of value to the group, and none should be made to feel out of place or foolish. Let the discussion flow from a spirit of trust and concern and from your own willingness to share something of yourself.

Opening Worship

Pray together, **Heavenly Father, we thank You for bringing us together to study Your Word. In Genesis we first learn of Your great love for Your people, of Your mercy and Your patience. We thank You that Your steadfast love and mercy have continued throughout all generations. For the sake of Your Son, You have forgiven us our sins and restored our relationship to You. Help us reflect Your love to others so that we may live in peace and unity. Amen.**

The Class Session

Read quickly through the Introduction and the Overview in the Study Guide. Ask the class if they have anything to add from their own reading of these chapters.

Under each of the sections in the Study Guide marked Focus 1 and Focus 2 are three items for discussion. You might consider dividing your class into three groups and letting each group have some time to study one of the subjects under each heading. Then bring everyone together to share their thoughts. Or, you might read through the discussion items and choose those items that are of greatest interest.

Focus 1: Roots

1. **Gen. 1:26–27; 2:4–8;** and **2:21–22** tell us that the roots of humanity are in God. As you discuss this section, the emphasis should be on the unique gift of life to each person and the root of that life in God. We are God's beloved creation. We have a direct connection with the Divine and a worth beyond anything we could create out of ourselves. Life is a gift from God. Life and death belong in the province of God. Therefore, no individual has a right to take human life apart from the instrument (government) God has instituted to provide peace and well-being in society (see **Rom. 13:1–6**). You might want to discuss abortion, war, capital punishment, and "mercy" killing.

2. **Gen. 1:28–31** and **2:8–14.** The emphasis is on our place in the world. We are creatures. We belong in God's world. We are listed scientifically as animals, but we are different from the rest of the created animal world in that we are set apart by a life-breathed process of creation and a relationship to God that is marked by love and responsibility.

3. **Gen. 2:15–17.** Man was originally given free will, which set him apart. We are not robots made to carry out the whim of the Creator. Adam and Eve were children of God, made in His likeness, given the right and responsibility to choose to serve. Sin later corrupted the will of humanity. We no longer freely choose to serve God, but He chooses us in Christ and by His Spirit moves us to serve Him and others.

Focus 2: Relationships

Just as our deepest roots are exposed in **Genesis,** so are our fundamental relationships. St. Augustine expressed it well in his *Confessions:* "Thou hast made us for Thyself, O Lord, and our hearts are restless until they rest in Thee." Only a loving relationship with God can make us whole and complete. Losing that relationship (as the next lesson will show) destroys also our joyful, loving relationship with other people. Losing our roots in God means that we bring forth the bitter fruits of hate, jealousy, lust, greed, and all the rest.

1. **Gen. 1:26–27; 2:4–8;** and **2:21–22.** Our fundamental relationship is

to God. It is the relationship of Creator to creature. It sets us in the order of belonging in the world and gives our life meaning. The disruption of this relationship by sin causes us agony in a life that becomes meaningless and bound for destruction. People act out that painful lostness in a kind of frantic running about, seeking meaning in experience or in homemade gods. You might spend some time talking about that fruitless search for "God" in life, which seems to consume so many.

2. **Gen. 2:4–9** stresses that the world was created *for* man. He has dominion over the earth. To some people, dominion suggests that people have the right to do anything they want with the earth, making the earth a means of self-enrichment through exploitation. Discuss the ways in which we responsibly carry out dominion.

3. **Gen. 2:20–24.** This portion can be discussed in conjunction with number 2 below. Eve is formed from Adam's rib—she is part of him. When husband and wife become one flesh in the marriage relationship, they manifest this oneness.

Creation Now

These discussion questions are designed to deal with concerns that might arise out of the study of **Genesis** as we live our life.

1. The emphasis is on the worth of humankind. It is neither biblical nor human to see humankind or one's self as worthless. That sense of worthlessness is destructive. Keep this discussion positive. Let those who are willing share their feelings of worthlessness. Bring the Word of God to bear on their feelings and remind those who experience that kind of emptiness that we were bought back to a proper Creator/creature relationship with God at a great price—Jesus' death on the cross.

2. This is an opportunity to discuss the male/female relationship in more detail. You will miss the beauty of the **Genesis** concept, however, if you misunderstand and distort the God-ordained roles for men and women set forth here. It is a distortion to infer from this that man is created as "master" or "owner" of woman. Rather, men and women enjoy a unique oneness with one another, fulfilling that oneness when they complement and live as "helpers" to one another. Read **Eph. 5:21–33** and **1 Peter 3:1–7.** Allow time for sharing the kinds of things that threaten the oneness in marriage. Return to the truth that our relationships must be rooted in God's forgiveness and grace in Jesus Christ.

Closing Worship

Sing or speak the following stanzas from "Praise to the Lord, the Almighty."

Praise to the Lord, the Almighty, the King of creation!
O my soul, praise Him, for He is your health and salvation!
Let all who hear Now to His temple draw near,
Joining in glad adoration!

Praise to the Lord! Oh, let all that is in me adore Him!
All that has life and breath, come now with praises before Him!
Let the amen Sound from His people again.
Gladly forever adore Him!

Lesson 2

Something Happened (Genesis 3–4)

Preparation for This Lesson

1. Read **Genesis 3–4**. Have a Bible commentary handy to check any verses that you have trouble understanding.

2. Study the lesson material in the Study Guide and in the Leaders Notes. Note important questions for discussion.

3. Scan the genealogy in **Gen. 5:6–32**. Display the Genesis Family Tree (at the end of this book) in your class area. Be prepared to add the additional names.

4. Prepare for worship, or ask someone from your class to be worship leader for the session.

Before the Session Begins

Again, take time to build relationships. Ask a volunteer or two to tell something that has happened to them over the past week.

Opening Worship

Pray, **Gracious Father, You created humanity in Your image and gave Adam and Eve every good and gracious gift. But their disobedience of Your will destroyed the perfect relationship they had enjoyed with You in the Garden. Your love for Your creation endured even then, and You promised a Savior who would come and deliver Your people from the bondage of Satan. You were faithful** to that promise, and for this we thank and praise You. Amen.

The Class Session

You could begin your class with a brief discussion of snakes. Most will probably indicate revulsion at the thought of snakes, and you can connect that with the cultural training we have had that marks snakes as evil. Lead from that discussion to a reading of the Introduction and the Overview of the lesson in the Study Guide. Stop at any time for items that need discussion or explanation. Try to encourage open sharing on the material presented. You might ask, "How does this make you feel?" after you have read the Overview. The feeling of gloom will be dealt with again later in the lesson.

If there is interest, use class time to read and discuss portions of Scripture that are suggested by members of the class.

Focus 1: Roots—Who Is to Blame?

The purpose of the section is that participants realize that as it was not possible for Adam and Eve to set aside the responsibility for their acts, so we cannot be free from our own guilt by blaming someone else. Who is to blame? We all are.

1. The tree was not at fault. It was part of God's perfect creation. The disobedience and therefore the "fault" was man's. The tree is like many things on earth given to us. They are treasures when they are used according to God's will, but they become curses when we twist them and try to make them serve us and our own will, apart from God's purposes.

2. **Revelation** names the serpent as Satan, and we find more about Satan in the book of **Revelation** than in **Genesis.** Here he is a serpent, set on deceiving man and woman. Later portions of Scripture show him to be the prince of darkness, set to destroy God's world and especially to destroy the life and faith of the believer. Peter calls him a "roaring lion"—surely a more frightening picture than that of a snake.

3. Eve wanted to be like God—to know good and evil. She did find out about evil; she experienced it firsthand. Her sin began not with the eating, but with the pride that made her seek to be like God and the lack of faith that led her to doubt God's word and promise.

4. Adam's defense is classic and useless. "I did it because You gave her to me and she made me do it." Adam tries to fix the blame on someone else. We still do that when we are unwilling to take responsibility for our acts.

Focus 2: Relationships—What Happened as a Result?

1. The initial consequences were shame, guilt, blame—internal destruction. First the two sinners show shame at being naked. They seek to hide from God, because they cannot bear to have Him look at them. They cover themselves. We still cover ourselves with masks of goodness that we hope will show the world that we are not sin-sick and evil. People cannot expose themselves to one another, much less to God, because they are ashamed.

There was also guilt. Adam and Eve knew they had sinned, and they tried to escape. We still run from our guilt and try to hide so that we will not have to face what we are and what we have done.

There was also blame. Adam and Eve tried to blame everyone else, even God, as though He were somehow responsible. All their effort does nothing to remove the result of sin—the internal pain and guilt that wear us down and eventually destroy us.

2. The physical consequences were broken relationships; childbearing became painful; the woman comes under the control of the man; man is set at war with himself and his environment. He must battle with the ground for food and eventually die. We too still suffer pain and strive to make a living, and still we die.

3. The cause of Cain's murder of Abel is sin. Cain cannot pass off the murder, and he cannot make God responsible. Cain's attitude has become corrupt, and it is his anger **(4:6–7)** that first implicates him and then brings him to the point of murder, for which he must suffer the consequences.

Cain's question, "Am I my brother's keeper?" is clearly the attitude brought about by sin in every person. We don't want to be responsible—to be involved in someone else's life and problems. It is that noncaring distance between people that makes violent acts possible. The distance is so far that only the healing forgiveness of God in Christ can overcome it.

4. The descendants of Cain go about their lives, apparently out of contact with God, doing their living and their raising of children. Lamech is proud of his self-reliance and glories in his acts of murder and violence. Things have not changed much.

Creation Now

1. This is a good time to discuss the Gospel of Jesus Christ. It is the only answer we have to the gloomy and devastating picture of sin, separation, and destruction. Salvation is promised in the verses indicated, and it is fulfilled in the death and resurrection of Jesus Christ. For the Christian this portion of Scripture reveals the nature of sin and its consequences for us.

It shows us once again our need for the forgiveness of God in Christ. It is our only escape.

2. The story of the fall does not excuse sin. God holds all the participants accountable for their actions. Sometimes we feel we cannot avoid doing wrong. But that does not excuse us. Rather Christ's work for us has secured God's pardon. Christ's death and resurrection assure us He has paid for all our sins. We do not do people a favor when we ignore or excuse their sin. Rather, we help them when we encourage them to accept responsibility for violating God's Law and to seek forgiveness in Christ. When they repent, we too must forgive them. We violate the spirit of God's forgiveness if we refuse to forgive those who have hurt us. God's forgiveness cost Jesus His life, and for us to forgive may cost us something—perhaps our pride, our sense of fairness, or our desire for revenge. It is not always easy to forgive. But God calls us to forgive, as He forgives us.

3. There is no escaping guilt. On our own, we cannot find a way to set aside our guilt. We Christians are blessed, because we can look at the stark reality of our sin and still know that we are not doomed by that sin. It was carried to the cross and there forgiven. We need not suffer the pain of unresolved guilt. "It is for freedom that Christ has set us free. Stand firm," writes St. Paul **(Gal. 5:1)**.

Closing Worship

Speak these stanzas from "All Mankind Fell in Adam's Fall."

As by one man all mankind fell
And, born in sin, was doomed to hell,
So by one Man, who took our place,
We all received the gift of grace.

We thank You, Christ; new life is ours,
New light, new hope, new strength, new pow'rs:
This grace our ev'ry way attend
Until we reach our journey's end.

Lesson 3
Beginning Again (Genesis 6–11)

Preparation for This Lesson

1. Read **Genesis 6–11,** concentrating on **6–9** and **11:1–9.** Use a Bible commentary to check questions. Select portions to read in class.

2. Study the lesson material in the Study Guide and in the Leaders Notes and decide what approach you will take and the points you will emphasize.

3. Scan the genealogies in **chapters 10** and **11:10–32.** Display the Genesis Family Tree in the back of this book and add the names in these portions of Scripture.

4. Get a picture or drawing of the ark and add the dimensions. It could serve as a center of attention for beginning discussion. Another option would be to ask the group members toread **6:14–16** and to draw a picture of the ark from the description.

5. Prepare for class worship or choose a class member to serve as worship leader.

Before the Session Begins

You might begin with an informal discussion of floods and recent accounts of floods. What is similar in all of them? How do they affect the relationships between the people involved? What good and bad behavior is usually found? What kinds of fear do people in a flood experience?

Move into a discussion of the flood in **Genesis.** Most of your class will have some knowledge of the flood, and you might read portions of **chapters 6–9** and talk about details of the flood. Use your picture(s) of the ark to emphasize God's miraculous salvation of Noah and his family.

Opening Worship

Pray, **Heavenly Father, You saw how great our wickedness on the earth had become and that our hearts were turned toward evil. You sorrowed that You had made us. Yet You showed Your grace toward Noah and his family, and in them You saved the world. Now we enjoy the living waters of Your refreshing love, given freely in Your Son. Your waters of Baptism have washed us clean and given us new life. Your rainbow reminds us that You always keep Your promises. Amen.**

The Class Session

Have the class read the Introduction. The Introduction centers on the faith act of Noah in completing his task. We obviously don't know what the reaction of the people of his time was, but building the ark on the basis of what Noah believed to be a revelation from God was a considerable act of faith. It might be a good time to discuss our own faith commitment.

You can use the Overview to get into the Scriptures or as a review after you have read the selected portions. It will alert the reader to certain themes or serve as a summary, centering on repeated themes.

Focus 1: Roots

In this section we seek our continuing roots as individuals in the accounts of the beginnings in **Genesis.**

1. Adam and Noah were both creatures of God; both were chosen for a task; both were weak and showed their sinfulness; both were promised salvation by the grace of God. We, like Noah, are counted righteous by faith.

2. The story of the Tower of Babel repeats many of the elements of the fall. Pride and arrogance again lead to trouble. God's judgment is rejected, and that leads to separation between man and God and erects barriers between man and man. You might want to discuss further the way sin breaks down communication between people.

3. Assign these questions to those in your group with a good biblical background and access to some Bible study helps. They should come to see that there is a similarity in the choosing of each person to perform a special task; the grace of God given to each to complete the task; the reluctance of most to respond to the call; the weakness of each; and the way in which the promises of God are carried out through each. These chosen people are forerunners of the Savior to come. Though imperfect, they point to the perfect, chosen Savior, Jesus of Nazareth, God's only begotten Son. He alone is the One who does not fail, the One who rescues each of us.

Focus 2: Relationships

1. The passage **6:1–4** is difficult to interpret. Just who the "sons of God" were is obscure. You might check a commentary for some possible explanations. The point of the section **(6:1–12)** is that man continued in the sin that Adam and Eve began, and that sinfulness showed itself in much the same way it does now.

2. If you have not done so, describe the ark and the flood. Make the point that God takes sin seriously. The discussion of this item might be

done in connection with number 2 under Creation Now.

3. The emphasis in the flood account is on God's washing away sinners except those whom He had chosen by grace to live. We are chosen to be His people in Baptism. For this reason Scripture says that just as Noah and his family were saved through the flood, so we are saved through Baptism **(1 Peter 3:20–21)**. Our faith life is the living out of our calling by God to be His own in Christ. Just as Noah was given the task of being God's instrument to save the chosen, so our task is to proclaim the Gospel, which gives eternal life and salvation.

4. This item might be assigned to an individual or small group for later reporting. The idea of covenant—the relationship between God and man founded on God's grace—will come up often in this study. It is necessary to have a clear picture of what God's covenant was and what it meant to the Israelites in the Old Testament. God came to Abraham and commanded him to go to "the land I will show you." He gave to him this promise: "I will bless those who bless you, and whoever curses you I will curse; and all peoples on earth will be blessed through you" **(Gen. 12:1–3)**. Repeatedly God renews this promise to Abraham. Abraham believed this promise, and it was credited to him as righteousness **(Rom. 4:22)**. In faith Abraham and his descendants looked forward to the coming of the Messiah, who would suffer and die for their sins. Like the old covenant with Abraham, Jesus' new covenant is a free gift for our benefit, sealed with the sacrifice of His own life on the cross. It requires no obedience on our part to complete the contract. The work of salvation is complete in Him. Just as in the old covenant, so also we in the new covenant are called to a life of obedience in response to God's steadfast love and forgiveness.

Creation Now

1. This item offers the opportunity to discuss Baptism as a complete act of salvation to us as individuals. Paul says we are "buried with Him through baptism into death" **(Rom. 6:4)**. Martin Luther, in his Small Catechism explanation of Baptism, expands that interpretation to a "daily" drowning of the Old Adam in us. Talk about the way in which the drama of the flood and Baptism with all of the themes mentioned is lived out every day in the life of the Christian as we struggle with sin, live as "sinner and saint" at the same time, and constantly return to the forgiveness of God to be "washed" of our sin and rededicated to Him.

2. It is a good time to deal realistically with the discomfort that some in your class may feel with the picture of God as the Judge who destroys life. We like to see God as a loving Father. We tend to ignore, or refuse to face, the judgment of God. But we must maintain with Jesus that God indeed

hates sin. Jesus Himself vigorously condemns the sins of arrogance and pride that He encountered **(Matthew 23)**. We do not easily accept this part of God's revelation of Himself. But we must, for if God does not take sin seriously, if He sets it aside in a careless way, then Jesus' death on the cross is a sham. The seriousness of sin makes the cross necessary. The punishment for sin—death and eternal damnation—makes our need for salvation in Jesus Christ total. We do not receive from God a spiritual pat on the head. We are involved in a desperate rescue from destruction—a destruction that is coming as surely as destruction came to the people of Noah's day.

Closing Worship

Sing or speak the following stanzas of "Salvation unto Us Has Come."

Salvation unto us has come By God's free grace and favor;
Good works cannot avert our doom, They help and save us never.
Faith looks to Jesus Christ alone, Who did for all the world atone;
He is our one Redeemer.

Faith clings to Jesus' cross alone And rests in Him unceasing;
And by its fruits true faith is known, With love and hope increasing.
For faith alone can justify; Works serve our neighbor and supply
The proof that faith is living.

All blessing, honor, thanks, and praise To Father, Son, and Spirit,
The God who saved us by His grace; All glory to His merit.
O triune God in heav'n above, You have revealed Your saving love;
Your blessed name we hallow.

Part II Patriarchal History

Lesson 4
The Father of the Nation (11:31–14:24)

Preparation for This Lesson

1. Read **Gen. 11:31–14:24.** You might use a paraphrase edition of the Bible and check a commentary to help you understand difficult portions. A commentary would be particularly helpful in dealing with **14:17–20.**

2. Study the lesson material in the Study Guide and in the Leaders Notes. Select the portions of Scripture and the topics or themes on which you want your group to concentrate.

3. Try to secure a large map of the ancient near east (or use maps in the back of your Bible) in order to understand Abram's place of origin and his travels.

4. Prepare for your class worship or select a worship leader.

Before the Session Begins

Try some relationship-building activities again. Let the class have some time to talk about how some of the insights gained from this study have influenced their lives. Have they seen things in a different way? Has their Baptism, or their personal covenant with God, become more meaningful? Are there things they have studied or learned that have been troublesome? Allow them to share in an atmosphere of trust and acceptance. If some have not studied **Genesis** before, they may have difficulty with some of the concepts and ways in which God reveals Himself. Give time and opportunity to work through these in the group. It is not the purpose of the study to judge someone's faith. The goal of this study, and of any study of Scripture, is that the Spirit will work through the Word to strengthen faith.

Opening Worship

Pray, **Dear Father in heaven, You called Your servant Abraham to travel to a foreign land. He obeyed Your call, trusting Your promise to make him a blessing to all peoples. You sometimes ask us to journey in Your name to places we do not care to go. Help us to** remember that You are always with us. Make us willing travelers along Your path and forgive us when we are not eager to obey Your call and follow You; in Jesus' name. Amen.

The Class Session

If there are individuals or groups that have done research suggested from the last session, allow them to present their findings. Their insights on these men of faith of the Old Testament and on the covenant will be helpful in this session. If you have not assigned those topics, it might be good to review the concept of covenant and the elements that constituted a covenant, and then relate that information to formal or legal contracts of today.

The lesson material centers on God's dealing with the man Abram (later called Abraham—"father of many"). Abram was "chosen" and made a part of a special covenant.

The Introduction will help participants experience the original encounter between God and Abram and make that encounter more real. The Overview can lead into the biblical material you have chosen to read, or it can serve as a summary after the parts of the lesson you have selected have been completed.

Focus 1: Roots

1. The passages mentioned (12:7–9; 13:14–17) are used by some Jewish people to claim the land of Palestine. This tiny portion of land has been contested as long as history has been recorded.

The claim of being Abraham's descendants was an Israelite claim to possess the special blessings and grace of God. They were God's chosen people. But some abused this position of privilege. In Jesus' day some Jews arrogantly claimed they didn't need Christ because of their ancestors (John 8:31–59). Our spiritual roots are in Abraham, because he became the father of all believers—God's chosen people in all ages and all generations. You might suggest that one or more of the class members read Romans 1–8 and see how the early church and Paul dealt with the unique claim of the Jews that the Old Testament law was sacred and binding, and how the "new law" of salvation in Jesus Christ superseded it. If they are willing, ask for a report to the class.

2. The map will help with this item. Show how Palestine is centrally located in the known world of that day. It was a highway around the desert, a center of culture and communication. The area was a vital link between the great civilization of Egypt and that of Babylon, Syria, and Persia. It was the perfect place for the chosen people of God and a perfect

place for the coming of the Savior when the time was right.

Focus 2: Relationships

1. If you did not do so in the Introduction to the lesson, review the concept of covenant now. Read **12:1–3, 7,** and **13:14–17.** Find the covenant elements in this promise: God promises (1) the Promised Land; (2) many descendants to fill the land; (3) a great blessing to come from the descendants, who will be a blessing to all. This promise is not given as a response to the "goodness" of Abram, but it is a gracious act of God. In Christ we are offered a "promised land" as well, also freely without merit on our part. We inherit, by the merit of Christ, the promised salvation, the kingdom of heaven.

2. If you have a group appointed to report on the comparison of the Old Testament "men of faith" from last session, it might be good to allow them to make the comparison of Abraham to that "chosen" group. If you did it as a class exercise, refer back to session 3, number 3, under Roots, and compare Abraham on the basis of the questions there. He was also a "savior"— a chosen one. Through him the promises of God reached His people. Also, he sometimes failed.

3. Abram was a "good" man. He showed the marks of faith that we seek today. He worshiped God; he shared his wealth; he was concerned about his family and neighbors; and he was kind. He would certainly be recognized as a "man of faith" today.

4. Read **Hebrews 7.** The points of comparison between Melchizedek and Christ apparently are as follows: (1) Melchizedek is king and priest as is Christ; (2) Melchizedek is called "king of righteousness" and "king of peace" as was Christ; (3) Christ is a priest after the order of Melchizedek rather than after the tribe of Levi, the tribe of all the other Old Testament priests. Christ is, therefore, of a "new" priesthood—not bound by the Old Testament ceremonial law. We have access to God, not through the Levitical law, but through our Lord Jesus Christ.

Creation Now

1. The account in **12:10–19** shows a weakness in Abram.He trusted God enough to go where he was told but not enough to believe that God would preserve his life. And so he also brings the legacy of the fall—sin and judgment. The account emphasizes once again that God does not choose people on the basis of their own goodness or strength. He is not selecting only those able to do His will. It does no good to try to ignore God's purpose for our life by using the excuse that we are not "good" enough. The Bible is filled with examples of God using people, with their faults and failings, to

become instruments of His grace (Samson, Gideon, Peter, etc.). We cannot plead inability. Our ability is from God.

2. A careful discussion of the relationship between faith and the action of faith we call "works" is in order. It can be emphasized that the "works" of faith—the evidence of faith in our life—are expected. But our works are not the cause of God's grace, nor are they the means by which it comes to us. He comes by His own choice, by the means He has established—His Word and sacraments. The accounts of Abraham and the other early believers show that the action is always first from God; then they respond. Our attempts at goodness are the witness to our faith and the way we let our light shine. We must be careful not to make those who struggle with their faith, or in whom faith is weak, despair over their inability to live up to the standard of goodness that seems to have been set up for them. The working of faith is always in terms of the power given us by God in the context of His forgiveness when we fail.

Closing Worship

Sing or speak the following stanzas from "The God of Abraham Praise."

The God of Abr'am praise, Who reigns enthroned above;
Ancient of everlasting days And God of love.
Jehovah, great I Am! By earth and heav'n confessed;
I bow and bless the sacred name Forever blest.

The goodly land I see, With peace and plenty blest;
A land of sacred liberty And endless rest.
There milk and honey flow, And oil and wine abound,
And trees of life forever grow With mercy crowned.

The whole triumphant host Give thanks to God on high.
"Hail, Father, Son, and Holy Ghost!" They ever cry.
Hail, Abr'am's God and mine! I join the heav'nly lays:
All might and majesty are Thine And endless praise!

Lesson 5
Some Laughable Promises (Genesis 15–20)

Preparation for This Lesson

1. Read **Genesis 15–20.** Use a Bible commentary to help you with difficulties.

2. Work through the material in the Study Guide and in the Leaders Notes. Plan your session time so that you can concentrate on those items that you think are important.

3. Prepare a chalkboard or poster board for today's presession activity as described below.

4. Make preparation for today's worship.

Before the Session Begins

Write on a chalkboard or poster board the phrase "Faith is . . ." Below this phrase write the following:

1. Trusting God completely at all times.

2. Believing that God will fulfill His promises to me, even if I sometimes doubt.

3. Knowing God's will for me and living according to it.

As participants enter, ask each person to place a check mark beside the definition of faith that seems most correct. Try to encourage each person to choose just one. Don't add definitions at this time.

When all participants are present, discuss these definitions of faith and ask for reasons why certain definitions were chosen. Don't try to get agreement. After 5 or 10 minutes of discussion continue with the Introduction in the Study Guide.

Opening Worship

Pray, **Almighty God, You showed Your servant Abraham the night sky and asked him to count the stars. You promised him that his offspring would be as numerous as the stars. Abraham, though he was childless, believed You, and his faith was credited to him as righteousness. Thank You for the gift of faith in Your Son, our Savior. Your blessings are indeed as countless as the stars. We are now clothed with Christ's righteousness and bold to stand before You. Keep us faithful to You and Your Word. Amen.**

The Class Session

The Introduction focuses on the faith of Abraham. Read it in conjunction with the Overview and then refer back to the definitions of faith. What would Abraham's definition be? Abraham would probably choose definition 2. We would add that God fulfills His promises through Jesus Christ as revealed in the Holy Scriptures. After reading the Overview you may wish to read those portions of the Scripture section that you have chosen as important.

Focus 1: Roots

1. The passages indicate doubt, blaming God, sexual relationships outside of marriage, mistrust of the promises of God, cruelty, scorning God, reluctance to leave sinful places, incest, and others. The evidence for the continuing presence of original sin is overwhelming. The people fail again and again. It would be good to stress the continuing patience of God in the face of these evil acts. He stands by His choice and does not abandon his chosen ones in their weakness. We should remember that this is forgiveness. He is not overlooking their sin. Sin is still serious **(chapter 19)**, but He does forgive.

2. The passages repeat the giving and choosing actions of God over and over again in the covenant. God is shown reaching beyond the limits of human concern, showing pity and mercy to His creatures. The evidence of God's "steadfast love," His self-giving love, is shown here in promises of a coming Savior, Jesus Christ, through whom all the families of the earth are blessed (**Gen. 12:3**).

3. The Sodom and Gomorrah event recalls the flood. It would be interesting to compare the two **(Genesis 6–7; 19)**. These themes are alike: (a) the wickedness of man brings about God's judgment; (b) God acts to save a "remnant"; (c) God destroys by a spectacular event, but His chosen ones escape. You might also point out areas of difference: (a) here the sin is specified **(18:20; 19:4–5)**; (b) the destruction is by burning sulfur, not water; (c) while the flood ends on a note of hope for re-creation, there is no indication of rebuilding here.

Focus 2: Relationships

1. It might be helpful to divide the class into three groups and assign each group one of the "covenant promise" accounts. After they have had time for small-group study, bring them together and let a "reporter" from each group discuss their account in terms of what is promised and Abraham's reaction. Here are some guidelines to help you work with the groups:

15:1–18. *The promise:* great reward; many descendants; Abraham will possess the land; specific borders of the land are identified. *Abraham's response:* he believed the Lord but asked for a sign (faith and doubt).

17:1–27. *The promise:* many nations will come from Abraham's descendants; Abraham and his descendants will possess the land of Canaan; Sarah will have a son the following year. *Abraham's response:* disbelieving laughter; circumcision of all males in the household in obedience to God's command (doubt and faith).

18:1–15. *The promise:* Sarah will have a son the following spring. *Abraham's response:* not indicated, but this time Sarah laughs in disbelief.

Other information that might be discussed in connection with the covenant:

a. The land promised in **15:18–21** was not completely possessed until the reign of Solomon, and it was held only for a short time. Disobedience again caused the loss of the Promised Land.

b. In **17:1–26** names are changed: Abram to Abraham (father of many) and Sarai to Sarah (princess). Recall that naming denotes rule. By naming these bearers of the covenant, God affirmed His rule in their lives.

2. Sarah blames God for her barrenness and tries to solve the problem of a descendant herself by giving Hagar to Abraham. He goes along, as docile as Adam eating the forbidden fruit. Then Sarah regrets her act and eventually drives Hagar out because of jealousy. God intervenes and saves Hagar and her unborn son.

3. There is real danger in living with those who are engaged in outward sinfulness. It is very difficult not to be affected and get involved. Talk about the importance of good "influencers" in our lives, even when we are adults. Lot's wife could not tear herself away from the place, even though it was evil, and she met the judgment of God.

4. This event is a "replay" of the account in **12:10–20.** Abraham still cannot believe that God will spare his life. He wants to make sure himself. Again there is sin, judgment by God, an act of saving in which God encounters and warns the king as He removes the impending punishment.

Creation Now

1. Abraham offers a good backdrop against which to look at our own doubt. Doubt can reveal a weak faith or the sin of unbelief. But doubt is not removed by louder pronouncement. It does help, however, to share the doubt and to see that the doubt we suffer is not unique. The Holy Spirit works through the Word of God to help us overcome our doubt. We should confess our doubt and make use of the means of grace, which God has provided to strengthen our faith. Get suggestions from the class about how

they handle doubt. Assure those who struggle that God is as patient with them as He was with Abraham and with Thomas. He constantly calls us back to Him in Christ and offers us, again and again, the forgiveness and strength we need.

2. You might want to make this a class activity and write the answers on the board. Here are suggested answers:

a. God has promised salvation **(John 3:16).** That is, He has assured us of eternal life with Him. He has also promised forgiveness through the same sacrifice of Christ.

b. He has done it out of his infinite love for us. It is a love demonstrated here with Abraham and a love that glows brightly throughout Scripture.

c. Jesus' death on the cross and His resurrection are the "seal" of the new covenant—the assurance that the gifts will be given.

d. The gifts are received by faith, but even faith itself is a gift. God works faith in us through the Sacraments and the Word, and by faith we are able to serve Him **(Eph. 2:8–10).**

e. God's covenant with Abraham promised both material blessings and most especially the great spiritual blessings of the coming Messiah. Our covenant in Christ looks back to the blessings of forgiveness, life, and salvation, which were won for us and for all people through the Messiah, who came according to God's promise.

Closing Worship

Ask for several volunteers to offer short prayers thanking God for His faithfulness to His covenant with Abraham and with us.

Lesson 6

And Now the Good News (Genesis 21–23)

Preparation for This Lesson

1. Read **Genesis 21–23.** You will want to check one or more Bible commentaries concerning God's test of Abraham in **chapter 22.**

2. Work through the material in the Study Guide and in the Leaders Notes. Choose the items you wish to emphasize with the class.

3. Be sure the Genesis Family Tree found at the end of this book is displayed so that Isaac's name can be added.

4. Plan your class worship.

Before the Session Begins

Display the Genesis Family Tree. It has been some time since a new name has been added. The pause illustrates the long wait Abraham had for Isaac, his promised heir. Take a little time to share thoughts about the meaning of waiting for the promises of God. What experiences have members of the group had while waiting for God? What kinds of feelings did they experience during those times of waiting? Might some of Abraham's doubt be connected to that long time of waiting?

Opening Worship

Pray, **Gracious Father, You blessed Sarah and Abraham with a son, and so began to fulfill Your promise to make Abraham the "father of many." This child Isaac was their great joy, and yet Abraham was obedient to Your harsh command that he sacrifice to You the son he loved. In Your mercy You saved Isaac's life and provided a sacrifice in his place. For us, You have also provided the perfect sacrifice of Your Son, whom You love, and by His death and resurrection we inherit eternal life. For that, we thank and praise You. Amen.**

The Class Session

Read through the Introduction and the Overview at the beginning of the class to set the stage for the events in the biblical text. Take some time to read through the account in **22:1–14** as the central focus of this section. If you want to concentrate your discussion on this event, use discussion questions number 1 under Roots and numbers 2 and 3 under Relationships.

Focus 1: Roots

1. Abraham loved God so much that he was willing to sacrifice his son in response to God's command. This scene is a picture of the way God loves us. God's love is not a distant favorable disposition toward us. God gives His own Son on the cross! Help the group talk about the meaning of the love of God in **John 3:16.**

2. The account in **23:1–20** carefully establishes Abraham's roots in the land. He bought the land for his wife's grave. He did not steal it. His claim to the Promised Land is not only based on the promise of God, but it is backed by a legitimate legal claim—a purchase. Once Sarah was buried there, the roots were planted. Israel belonged in Palestine.

3. Try to help the group realize that the "protector" or "helper" God is a

strong theme in the Old and New Testaments. One reason the leaders at Jesus' time did not recognize Jesus as the Messiah was that they had apparently forgotten that helping and serving was an important facet of God's dealing with His people. In the **Isaiah** passages, the Messiah is clearly pictured as the helper of those who are oppressed and in need. You might discuss how Jesus lived out that promise and why He used the words He did to show that He was the Messiah.

Focus 2: Relationships

1. **Gen. 21:1–8** is the fulfillment of the oft-repeated promise to Abraham. The fact that Isaac is born in the couple's old age says that God fulfills His promises in His own time. We can expect God to hear and answer—to keep His promises—but He will do so in His own time. "He laughs" apparently refers to the laughing Abraham and Sarah did when Isaac was promised.

2. The passages in **12:10–13** and **20:11–13** show Abraham as frightened and determined to save his own skin. They do not show a man of particular courage or integrity. Yet he is able to overcome his weakness, with the help of God, and show his faith by his willingness to perform the most difficult task. Paul struggled with his own inability to do what he knew God wanted him to do. We should encourage one another in our faith, pointing to the power of God that is ours in Jesus Christ.

3. Parents in particular should be able to identify the feelings of fear, pain, doubt, and finally relief. You might also talk about the infinite faith Isaac shows in his father. How is that like or unlike our relationship to parents today? Our relationship to God, if it would be like Abraham's, must be strengthened by the power of God through Word and Sacrament. And if our relationships of parent to child and child to parent would be perfected, they must exist under the grace of God and be constantly renewed by His forgiveness in Christ.

4. Abraham was a man of integrity in dealing with his neighbors. Because others are dishonest or outside the family of faith does not give us the right to ignore them or to mistreat them.

Creation Now

If you have time, read some of the suggested Scripture readings about Samson, Gideon, and Peter. If you only have time for one, choose Peter. The point of each—and a strong message in the story of Abraham—is that God works miracles *through* people, not because the people have some inner gifts or talents or training, but because He fits them to His purpose and fills them with the faith and power necessary to complete the task. It is both a comfort for us and an accusation. We can be assured that if we are chosen by God for a task, He will give us the Spirit and power to accomplish it. On the other hand, if we refuse God's call to service, our excuse can never be a lack of ability or talent or training. God supplies the equipment to do the task.

Again, remind participants that we live and move and act under the grace of God in Christ, which creates faith in us and forgives us when we fail.

Closing Worship

Sing or speak these stanzas from "Jesus, Still Lead On."

Jesus, still lead on Till our rest be won;
And although the way be cheerless,
We will follow calm and fearless;
Guide us by Your hand To our fatherland.

When we seek relief From a longfelt grief,
When temptations come alluring,
Make us patient and enduring;
Show us that bright shore Where we weep no more.

Jesus, still lead on Till our rest be won;
Heav'nly leader, still direct us,
Still support, console, protect us,
Till we safely stand In our fatherland.

Lesson 7

A Chosen Family (Genesis 24–26)

Preparation for This Lesson

1. Read **Genesis 24–26** with a commentary handy to check any difficult sections. Some further information on taking a vow **(24:2),** betrothal customs **(24:22, 53),** and marriage **(24:67)** might be helpful.

2. Work through the material in the Study Guide and in these notes and select those items you wish to emphasize. Choose portions of Scripture

that you will read in class.

3. Display the Genesis Family Tree at the end of this book. Add Jacob and Esau and the other named descendants of Abraham.

4. Plan today's worship or choose a worship leader.

Before the Session Begins

Much of today's session will be spent discussing family relationships. You might begin with discussion about modern stress on the family. Allow your group members to share personal difficulties if they wish to do so. Read over the Introduction as a way of beginning this discussion. Ask for responses to the conclusion in the Introduction. Why is it so difficult to live up to the ideal of the Christian home? You need not finish the discussion at the beginning of the class. You may complete it using the guidelines under Creation Now.

Opening Worship

Pray, **Dear Father in heaven, You have placed us in relationship with others—family, friends, neighbors, co-workers. You know our dealings with others are not always according to Your will. We ask Your forgiveness for the many times we fail to be kind and patient, especially to those in our family. Let Your forgiving love show us the way to forgive others. As You never forsook Abraham and Your chosen people, so abide with us and those we love, that our homes may reflect Your presence; in Jesus' name. Amen.**

The Class Session

Move into a reading of the Overview and the passages suggested there or others you have selected. Try to give the group a feeling for the movement of the story through the life of Isaac. Bring in any additional information you may have discovered in your research.

Focus 1: Roots

1. Warnings against intermarriage were given to preserve the covenant with God. The entire book of **Hosea** is a picture of God's relationship to His people in terms of the faithfulness and unfaithfulness of the nation of Israel as a wife to a husband. Idolatry is often compared to infidelity. Marriage in the Old Testament often meant practicing the religion of both marriage partners. Sharing the place of Yahweh with another god was unthinkable to the Israelites. Paul in **1 Cor. 7:10–18** seems to indicate that it would be better to marry one of the faith, but he considers it an opportunity for evangelism for those already married to unbelievers.

2. The parental choosing of marriage partners continued through Christ's time to the middle ages. Many today object to that system, because they feel that their individual rights are most important and because they have glorified the concept of romantic love as the basis for marriage. Families, also, no longer form alliances by marriages, nor are families generally rooted in a certain place.

3. The concept of the "chosen" was vital to the people of the covenant, because they believed the Messiah would come from the chosen family. The eldest of the chosen family inherited not only the property but also the right to be the ancestor (perhaps father) of the Messiah. God chose us to be His children by the Holy Spirit through Holy Baptism.

4. The passages compare Abraham to Isaac in parallel events. Both of them show weakness (they both try to save themselves by claiming their wife as their sister), and both of them show integrity and kindness in their agreements with Abimelech.

Focus 2: Relationships

1. Many examples of signs giving guidance are in Scripture—this is one of them. Although God may still give us signs, He has given us the Holy Scriptures to guide us. We must be careful, however, that we do not try to escape the responsibility for our life by expecting God to make our decisions for us. We cannot use "waiting for a sign" as an excuse for inaction. For the most part, we are given the faith and the strength **(Matt. 7:7)** to make our own decisions.

2. Isaac and Rebekah are unable to deal with the warring brothers. In this discussion, it is important to help parents recognize that it is "natural" to favor one child over another, at least sometimes. We need not punish ourselves with guilt about that. But it is also necessary to seek the grace of God to overcome any kind of favoritism that would hurt our children or make them jealous of one another.

3. The child of promise (often given to women who are barren: Sarah, Hannah, Elizabeth, and others) carries the meaning of the promise of the Messiah. The miracle of the birth is emphasized by the direct action of God. The theme of the "God-given" child culminates in the Child born to the Virgin Mary.

Creation Now

The discussion can center on the elements of a Christian home. Allow the members of the group to share some of their difficulties in living out their faith in their homes. Give understanding and encouragement to those who are struggling.

The impossibility of perfection does not mean that we should lose heart. The passages in **Ephesians** and **Colossians** outline some of the "Christian" elements of a home. Read them over and pick out as many as you can. Write them on the board and discuss them with the purpose of helping all to repent of past failures in these areas and to encourage them to seek help from God to improve.

Colossians emphasizes forgiveness. It is a good center for the discussion too. Isaac and Rebekah needed constant forgiveness, and so do we. While we seek the strength to live a life that is pleasing to God, we constantly need His forgiveness when we fail. It is only in the re-creating power of God's love in Christ that we find the strength to seek forgiveness from those around us as we forgive them.

Closing Worship

Sing or speak the following stanzas from "Oh, Blest the House."

Oh, blest the house, what'er befall,
Where Jesus Christ is all in all!
For if He were not dwelling there,
How dark and poor and void it were!

Oh, blest that house where faith is found
And all in charity abound
To trust their God and serve Him still
And do in all His holy will!

Then here will I and mine today
A solemn cov'nant make and say:
Though all the world forsake His Word,
My house and I will serve the Lord.

Lesson 8

It's Not My Fault (Genesis 27–28)

Preparation for This Lesson

1. Read **Genesis 27–28.** Check your commentary for explanations of

anything that is unclear to you. You might find it helpful to research information on *birthright* and *inheritance* in the Old Testament world.

2. Work through the lesson material in the Study Guide and in this Guide. Decide what points you wish to emphasize and how you will deal with the biblical material in the class.

3. Plan today's worship or select a worship leader.

Before the Session Begins

In this session you will want people to think through the whole area of the "rightness" and "wrongness" of their acts. You might begin the discussion by talking about some of the more flagrant examples of wrongdoing and deceit that have been in the news recently. You could discuss national affairs or local issues. In most cases the wrongdoers attempt to justify themselves by giving a good reason for their action (loyalty, self-preservation, concern for others). Help the class think about the implications of trying to find good reasons for our actions.

Opening Worship

Pray, **Father, Your servant Jacob deceived his father, Isaac. Still You blessed him and kept Your gracious promises first made to his grandfather Abraham. Forgive us when we seek to deceive others, and in Your mercy continue to bless us, even though we are undeserving. Thank You for Your Son, who always obeyed Your will perfectly, never seeking to deceive You or others. It was Your will that He die for the whole world so that we might be restored and live to Your glory, now and eternally. Amen.**

The Class Session

Go directly to the Introduction. It raises questions along the lines of the previous discussion. It suggests the arguments of those who try to justify every deed by giving a "loving" reason for it. You need not complete the discussion of this subject at this time. It will be dealt with under Creation Now.

Chapter 27 in particular lends itself to reading aloud. As you read, ask the group to think about how the people involved were feeling. What might have been some of the reasons they acted as they did? What evidences of breakdown in relationships can you see in the story?

Use the Overview as an introduction to the reading of the biblical portion or as a review after the reading.

Focus 1: Roots

Form four groups and assign one character to each. Emphasize that we are not just looking for good and bad behavior in these people, but also for changes in behavior and reasons for their actions. We want to discover truths to which we can relate.

Some guidelines for your groups:

Isaac appears to have been an obedient child and a gentle, obedient adult. He abides by the will of God and his own father and tries to live at peace with his neighbors. He shows some weaknesses in that he cannot seem to overcome the strife in his own house—though he surely must have tried—and he shows occasional signs of cowardice.

Rebekah at first seems to be a helpful girl. She goes out of her way to be kind, and she is obedient to her family and to her duty. Later she becomes almost shrewish—manipulating people, deceiving, and lying. She must have had a difficult time with her sons and with Esau's Canaanite wives.

Jacob appears to have been a gentle child, obedient to his mother, and religious. He does, however, cheat his brother and lie to his father. He seems to come off as resourceful and intelligent. He is the chosen one.

Esau does not seem to care much about things. He easily sells his birthright; he marries Canaanite women, apparently not even realizing that his parents don't like it; he bristles when he is taken advantage of and even plots to murder his brother.

These persons need help from God and others in order to go on. They are not perfect, but they are God's chosen ones. Like us, they struggle with their sinfulness. Their example shows us our need for forgiveness.

Focus 2: Relationships

1. The relationships suggest little communication or trust among the members of the family. Rebekah cannot go to Isaac with her problems. The root of much hurt in families lies in the lack of trust. You might discuss this item in conjunction with number 3 under Creation Now.

2. The fault is obviously shared. Rebekah and Jacob could both seek to justify themselves, but they must share the blame. We are to obey authority **(Rom. 13:1)**, except when it tells us to do something that violates the will of God. Then we must refuse to obey.

3. Sometimes the hurt in a family is deeper and more lasting than that among those outside of the family, because we expect better treatment from those who love us. We are hurt by their action and feel rejected and used. Jesus commands us to forgive 77 times, meaning times without number **(Matt. 18:21–22).** It is not easy.

4. God's promises do not depend on the persons to whom they are

given. God intended to carry out His promise to Abraham, and Jacob's misbehavior would not negate that intention. It means for us that God will not back out on His promises to love and forgive us, even when we stumble and fall. His love for us depends on Christ, not on us.

5. A vow to God (a pledge) can be good spiritual training, but it should not be done lightly. We are not required to make this kind of a pledge or promise. We may do it, however, in response to the goodness of God.

Creation Now

Both items 1 and 2 deal with the way we are to view the rightness and wrongness of our acts. In many cases we will find ourselves doing wrong. We don't have to even intend it—we just do it. Then we recognize that we need to repent and to receive God's forgiveness in Christ.

1. Sometimes we feel, however, that if we are trapped into doing wrong we can justify ourselves by giving a good reason for doing what we felt we "had to do." The whole approach sets us on the path of self-justification.

The point of this discussion should certainly not be to find some way to justify what we do—to find better reasons and excuses for ourselves. The point is that when we do wrong, for whatever reason, we must *not* try to justify ourselves. The self-justifying way of relating to God is sinful disobedience to Him. As soon as we think we can do the good, we are trapped into doing the bad **(Rom. 7:19).** We need to recognize that in each case we are not called upon to try harder to prove that we are "right," but we simply need to look to the cross of Christ for forgiveness. We cannot justify ourselves. It is Christ on the cross who justifies us. We cannot do "the right thing." We are trapped by our own sinfulness. We must seek Him and His salvation, or we are lost, no matter how good our intentions. Help the group understand that trying to justify certain acts is a dead end. We strive to obey God's will and to preserve the rights and feelings of others. When we fail, we turn again for forgiveness to Jesus Christ.

2. The end does not justify the means. When we do wrong, as Rebekah and Jacob did, we cling to the grace of God in Christ. We are expected to obey the Law. We cannot set it aside for a "good reason."

3. The discussion may be used as another look at the family relationship. The point here is connected with the items above. We may not think we need daily devotions to keep us "religious," but we need daily forgiveness to keep us together and whole. Stress the healing action that we can find in coming together to the cross of Christ to talk about our hurts and our needs, even our complaints. God loves and forgives us. We need to do the same for each other.

Closing Worship

Sing or speak the following three stanzas from "Dear Christians, One and All." This hymn has 10 stanzas, and together they tell the full salvation message of God's love and faithfulness. The second and third stanzas quoted here are Christ speaking to us.

The Son obeyed His Father's will,
Was born of virgin mother;
And God's good pleasure to fulfill,
He came to be my brother.
His royal pow'r disguised He bore,
A servant's form, like mine, He wore
To lead the devil captive.

"Though He will shed my precious blood,
Of life me thus bereaving,
All this I suffer for your good;
Be steadfast and believing.
Life will from death the vict'ry win;
My innocence shall bear your sin;
And you are blest forever.

"Now to My Father I depart,
From earth to heav'n ascending,
And, heav'nly wisdom to impart,
The Holy Spirit sending;
In trouble He will comfort you
And teach you always to be true
And into truth shall guide you."

Lesson 9
The Deceiver Is Deceived (Genesis 29–31)

Preparation for This Lesson

1. Read through **Genesis 29–31.** You will enjoy it—the people are fascinating. Use your commentary to help you with things you do not under-

stand. A look at ancient customs concerning marriage and children produced by concubines may be helpful for this lesson.

2. Study the material and the items for discussion in the Study Guide and in the Leaders Notes. Select those topics that seem most important to you. You might want to choose parts of the chapters of Scripture to read aloud. The section is too long to read all of it.

3. Display the Genesis Family Tree found at the end of this book.

4. Plan today's worship or select a worship leader.

Before the Session Begins

This would be a good time to review the Genesis Family Tree. As you review the names on the tree, focus especially on those who are the "chosen" ancestors of Christ. In today's session we study more about Jacob, but all of the "fathers" of the tribes of Israel are in this account.

Opening Worship

Pray, **In our Scripture reading for today, heavenly Father, we learn of the greed, dishonesty, and selfishness of both Jacob and Laban. Surely You grew weary of their games and foolishness. But You did not abandon Your covenant promises, and You continued to bless Jacob and his family with material wealth. For Your Son's sake, forgive us when we deal dishonestly or unfairly with others, when we put ourselves before others, when we put ourselves before You. Amen.**

The Class Session

You can move into your study of the text by reading the Introduction and the Overview. The major events in the biblical account are mentioned in the Overview. You might let the class select those events in the summary that seem most interesting to them and allow time to read aloud those Scripture sections.

Focus 1: Roots

1. Jacob and Laban make a pact or covenant with each other. It is a kind of healing act after their bitter argument. They still do not seem to trust each other, but they are able to let their mutual trust in God stand as a kind of sentinel between them. Their relationship was not happy, but the covenant agreement seemed to satisfy them. It was different than God's covenant in that it was an agreement between equals for the benefit of both. The agreement probably eased their anxiety about each other a little bit.

2. The consulting of "divination" is repeated in the Old Testament (**Ex. 7:11; Num. 22:6; 2 Kings 9:22; Dan. 5:7;** and others). It is condemned in **Lev. 19:26.** The household "gods" were household or family idols thought to serve as guardians of family property and inheritance. The people evidently had faith in them. God wants us to place our trust in Him, and in Him alone.

3. The names of all of the 12 tribes, except Benjamin, are here. It is interesting to note how much the names meant to their mothers. The names also became very important to the nation of Israel. After taking possession of the Promised Land, the tribe became part of a person's identity. It determined where one would live and often what kind of lifework one would do. Judah became the tribe of importance (especially after the captivity of the 10 tribes in 722 B.C.). It was the tribe of the "remnant" and the tribe from which the Savior was born.

Focus 2: Relationships

1. Both of the men involved misused the other. Jacob took advantage of Laban in that he manipulated the sheep (goats) to his advantage and ran off with much of what Laban owned. Laban tricked Jacob into marrying a wife he did not want, and then got him to work for many years, during which time Jacob made Laban a rich man. It is difficult to justify either. They both show that they are sinful. They are both proud. They both show the kind of selfishness and arrogance that got Adam and Eve into difficulty. We might advise them to repent and turn to the Savior. It is what we are called upon to do with our own sinful pride.

2. The complaining was the result of broken relationships and lack of love and trust. Complaining always speaks some kind of inner pain. It is, of course, often distorted by selfishness, but it can be a cry for help. Complaining is best dealt with not by ignoring it or putting it down, as we often do, but by hearing it and giving some reassuring love to the complainer.

3. It is difficult to follow the instructions in **Matt. 7:1–5.** We are not good at seeing our own faults nor ignoring the faults of others, especially those faults that affect us directly. We must constantly seek forgiveness for our judging and ask for the strength to accept people, even if we must reject their actions.

4. The theme is often repeated and lived out in the life of Christ. It became an identifying mark of the Messiah. See Lesson 6, Roots, number 3.

Creation Now

1. This discussion would be particularly helpful if you have people in the group who are actively involved in business and who are willing to discuss

their difficulties. The purpose is to lead people to repentance and faith so that they might receive forgiveness and the Spirit's power to lead a new life. God did not reject Jacob, despite all of Jacob's faults. He remained true to His promises. God does not reject us either. In Christ He calls us back when we fail.

2. Again, this is a subject for open discussion. It is certainly true that those who are constantly giving will be taken advantage of. At some point we must protect ourselves from being destroyed by the greed of others. It is very difficult to determine that point. It might be interesting to explore different ways Jacob might have handled his uncle's deception. Help the group to realize that loving and giving are always risky. They are our calling as followers of Christ.

3. There is nothing as important to the inner health of a person than to know that one is loved. An unloved child can become destructive to self and others. Leah shows that kind of self-pity, self-centeredness, and vengefulness that are symptoms of being unloved. Talk about ways to show love in families. What can we do when love becomes difficult? Talk about the need to go to God again and again for forgiveness in Christ. Assure everyone that, like giving, loving is a mission to which we are called by Christ and for which we are empowered by the Spirit. You might read through **1 Corinthians 13** in connection with this discussion.

Closing Worship

Sing or speak these stanzas from "My Hope Is Built on Nothing Less."

My hope is built on nothing less
Than Jesus' blood and righteousness;
No merit of my own I claim
But wholly lean on Jesus' name.
On Christ, the solid rock, I stand;
All other ground is sinking sand.

When He shall come with trumpet sound,
Oh, may I then in Him be found,
Clothed in His righteousness alone,
Redeemed to stand before the throne!
On Christ, the solid rock, I stand;
All other ground is sinking sand.

Lesson 10
Jacob Wrestles (Genesis 32–36)

Preparation for This Lesson

1. Read **Genesis 32–35.** Use your commentary to help you with difficult sections. **Chapter 36** contains a genealogy of the family of Esau. You might look it over and mention it to the group.

2. Study the materials in the Study Guide and in this Guide. Look over the discussion questions and decide which portions of Scripture you will read aloud in the class.

3. Plan your worship or choose a worship leader.

Before the Session Begins

By now the members of the group have probably developed a degree of trust in each other and should be able to talk about some of their more personal feelings. This session centers on Jacob's inner responses to the good and bad experiences of his life. You might ask the group members to talk about which person in **Genesis** has become most meaningful for them and why that person is special. Keep the discussion personal, but don't try to do any problem solving at this time. Talk and listen.

Opening Worship

Pray, **Merciful Father, Jacob wrestled with You and said, "I will not let You go unless You bless me." Because You are faithful, You blessed Jacob and gave him a new name. You have done the same for us in Baptism, giving us Your name and Your blessing. Help us to hold on to Your promise, never letting go of Your sure Word when the world and Satan would have us turn from You. Keep us faithful in our struggles of life and bless us for the sake of Jesus. Amen.**

The Class Session

Read through **32:22–30** before you read the Introduction. Give enough background to set the event. Then use the Introduction as a way of approaching this section of Scripture. Discussion can be completed under Creation Now.

Read through the Overview and read those portions of Scripture that you have selected or that seem important to the members of the class.

Focus: Roots and Relationships

We want to look at Jacob and the events of his life so that we can relate them to our own dealing with the joys and sorrows of life. The purpose is to gain some further insight into the working of God in our life.

1. Fear is universal. We constantly contend with fear. Most fears we try to ignore. Many we create for ourselves. Some people are almost incapacitated by their internal fears. Sometimes we are forced to face our fear, as Jacob was. How did he deal with his fear? Talk about the steps he took. How would they be practical guidelines for us in our dealing with fear? Make sure you don't play down fear, or pretend that fear is childish or foolish. Fear is real. It can only be overcome by recognizing it; admitting it; and asking the Holy Spirit to help us overcome it. We can gain comfort and strength when we remember Christ's promise never to leave or forsake us. Christians, sharing the promises of Christ, can strengthen and help one another through times of difficult fear.

2. Watch for people who grieve because of the separation of death, divorce, etc. You do not want to cause them pain. Keep the discussion positive and supportive. The pain in joy is that joy does not last long. The joy we can have even in the sadness of the death of a loved one is knowing that death is not final separation. Talk about ways in which believers can do what the passage in **Romans** suggests. What kinds of groups can we form, or what ways of being in contact with others can we establish, that will help us weep and rejoice with them? Talk about the message of the love of Christ that speaks to our times of weeping.

3. The disappointment we feel in others, especially in members of our family, is common. Somehow our love for ones close to us makes us expect great things of them. We have all felt the pain that comes when they let us down. Unfortunately, disappointment often leads to loss of respect, loss of love, and finally rejection. Many marriages and many parent-child relationships die in this way. Make it clear that even though Jesus grieved in disappointment in the people in Jerusalem, He did not stop loving them. We dare not let our love for others be conditioned by their behavior. We need to seek the help of God to style our love after His in Christ, an unconditional love.

There is a story about a minister who announced one Sunday after church that one of the members of the parish had been arrested for a serious crime. "I will be with him in court tomorrow," the pastor said. "If he is innocent, he will need me to defend him, and if he is guilty, he will need me to love him."

4. The temptation for some people is to worship God in times of crisis in short-term, quick-fix fashion. Worship continues until the problem goes

away. Help the class talk about the importance of worship as a response to the goodness of God as well as a response to the hardships of life. Worship serves God as it helps us grow through Word and Sacrament. It is within the worship context that we receive the abundant blessings He loves to give us—His forgiveness, His Supper, His strength. To worship God and to live a life of praise in His name is our greatest "work" as well as our greatest joy.

Creation Now

Don't get all bogged down in a discussion about who this "man" was. In the end, Jacob recognized that the man was God **(32:30)**. Jacob persisted, and eventually the man blessed Jacob. His name was changed to *Israel* (he who struggles with God).

We have, for the most part, lost the concept of "struggling" with God. We stress so much the necessity to be obedient to the will of God that we often seem to be apathetic in our approach to Him. Jesus compliments persistence of faith in the woman and the centurion.

Encourage the members of the class to confront the difficulties they have in feeling close enough to God to contend with Him and in feeling that they have the right to contend with Him. Remind them of the promises in **Matt. 7:7; 21:22; John 15:7;** and **16:24.** We are promised the resources we need to deal with the difficulties of life. We are not on our own. We are promised God's grace so that nothing "will be able to separate us from the love of God that is in Christ Jesus our Lord" **(Rom. 8:39)**.

Closing Worship

Sing or speak the following stanzas from "What a Friend We Have in Jesus."

What a friend we have in Jesus,
All our sins and griefs to bear!
What a privilege to carry
Ev'rything to God in prayer!
Oh, what peace we often forfeit;
Oh, what needless pain we bear—
All because we do not carry
Ev'rything to God in prayer!

Have we trials and temptations?
Is there trouble anywhere?
We should never be discouraged—

Take it to the Lord in prayer.
Can we find a friend so faithful
Who will all our sorrows share?
Jesus knows our ev'ry weakness—
Take it to the Lord in prayer.

Lesson 11
Meet a Hero (Genesis 37–41)

Preparation for This Lesson

1. Read **Genesis 37–41** with your commentary on **Genesis** available to check anything you do not understand.

2. Study the material in the Study Guide and in the Leaders Notes. Plan your approach to deal with those parts of the lesson and portions of Scripture that you consider to be the most important for your group.

3. Display the Genesis Family Tree (found at the back of this book) somewhere in your class area.

4. Plan today's worship or select a worship leader.

Before the Session Begins

Part of the lesson time today is spent on the difficult question concerning how our Christian lives are to be lived in the world. Are we to be so different that we become an accusation to others, or are we to be a part of the world, close to sinners so that we can relate to them in times of need? It is not an easy question, and the approach to people probably varies, but it is good to think through our present relationships. If possible, ask a pastor to talk about the response he gets when he is identified as a clergyman by a robe, clerical collar, or some other mark. He will probably reveal that some people are uncomfortable in his presence, even openly hostile. Some will ignore him, and some will show him special attention and favors. You can compare those responses to the way people react to "good" people. List the similarities.

Opening Worship

Pray, **Father in heaven, Your servant Joseph suffered injustice at the hands of his brothers, Potiphar's wife, and Potiphar himself.**

Throughout his ordeals, You continued to show Joseph Your favor and blessing. You made him a wise interpreter of dreams; You provided opportunities of leadership and responsibility; and You increased his patience and trust in You. Increase our faith and help us to resist temptation. Along with Joseph, give us courage to say, "How then could I do such a wicked thing and sin against God?" Forgive us for Your Son's sake when we fail. Amen.

The Class Session

Move immediately into the Introduction, which deals with the same subject. You may pause briefly for discussion or hold the discussion for the Creation Now section. The Introduction leads into the Overview, which you can also read. Stop to discuss matters of interest that come up. Read those parts of the Scripture that you have selected or that seem important to your class.

Focus 1: Roots

1. Most of the time this portion of **Genesis** is omitted from study because of its explicit sexuality, unflattering view of some of the patriarchs, and because it seems to interrupt the story of Joseph. If you think you will have time, read over the chapter and refer to **Matt. 1:1–17.** Pick out the names in this chapter that are in the genealogy. Several of the people mentioned in the family of Christ are in **chapter 38.** The sinless Son of God bore the sin and suffering of all, including His sinful ancestors, according to His human nature **(Heb. 2:10–18).** Again, the sinfulness of people cannot interfere with the plan of God.

2. There is no easy answer to the question about whether God reveals Himself in dreams today. Dream interpretation was very important at the time of Joseph, also at the time of Christ. It will not be possible to come to a final answer on this question. Don't spend a lot of time on it. It is important to remember that we are not to depend on dreams to know the will of God. His will for us is revealed in Christ and the Holy Scriptures. Any dream that contradicts that Word cannot be from God!

3. Joseph was a hero in that he seemed to live up to high standards of moral and ethical behavior expected. Most of the other people in **Genesis** are shown with glaring faults; Joseph is not. He would stand out in our day too. He points to Christ in a unique way in that the tradition of "holiness," being "set apart," became a part of the identification of the Messiah **(Is. 53:9).**

Focus 2: Relationships

1. The question deals with a situation that can be a problem for some families. The point of the discussion is to help those who feel the pressure of the "special" child deal better with that pressure. Parents of special children are torn between their desire to show pride in the talented child and their fear of hurting the other children in the family who seem less talented. The jealousy that the special child can create is also real and can be damaging. Talk about the responsibility of the special child to the family. Talk about the ways in which parents can affirm their other children as special, even though those children are obviously not as gifted as the special child. Most important, reaffirm the truth that sin destroys relationships. When we confess our sins, Jesus forgives them and heals relationships—between us and God and others. As a way of dealing with the question, you might talk about things Jacob could have done to avert the trouble that his special child caused.

2. The brothers are trapped into one sin by another. They see the result of their sin but cannot undo it. The point of the discussion is not just to condemn the sons of Jacob, but to help us when we find ourselves in similar situations. It is important that we go to the person we have hurt and seek forgiveness from that person **(Matt. 5:24)** and then repent and take our sin to God for forgiveness. And finally, it is important to leave the sin with God. To bear it as a load of guilt is a burden that the forgiveness of Christ does not make us bear.

3. All three responses occur, but it seems that people of the world often respond to honesty and integrity with hostility. The corruption of our nature makes us see goodness as an accusation of ourselves. It is like the hostility that Jesus and the prophets encountered. Yet we are to try, with God's help, to lead the life He would have us lead. We are assured that we have a home with Him in heaven and that nothing can take that away from us, no matter how difficult the people around us become.

Creation Now

Sadly, we will have to admit that often people are not able to identify us as Christian by our lives. Often we seem to blend with the world around us, and no one even notices us. We are fairly expert at "hiding our light under a bushel." On the other hand, aggressive goodness, the kind of "mission" or "evangelism" that does good things or speaks religious words because of the need of the doer or speaker and not of the person in need, can be just as destructive. We need to seek the gifts and grace of God to be more than invisible Christians and more than "do-gooders" for our own benefit. It is not possible to find a set of rules that will give us specific answers to each question that may arise. But as much as we are able, with God's help, we are to live a life of integrity, in accordance with the will of God as revealed in the Holy Scriptures. We are in the world around us as Jesus was, so that we will be there when friend or neighbor falls and seeks the help that we can give them in the Gospel of Jesus Christ. Part of our task as Christians is to live out the dilemma that we are in the world but not of the world.

Closing Worship
Sing or speak these stanzas from "What God Ordains Is Always Good."

What God ordains is always good:
His will is just and holy.
As He directs my life for me,
I follow meek and lowly.
My God indeed In ev'ry need
Knows well how He will shield me;
To Him, then, I will yield me.

What God ordains is always good:
He is my friend and father;
He suffers naught to do me harm
Though many storms may gather.
Now I may know Both joy and woe;
Someday I shall see clearly
That He has loved me dearly.

Lesson 12
A Change for the Better (Genesis 42–47)

Preparation for This Lesson
1. Read **Gen. 42:1–46:7** and **46:28–47:26.** Also, read the genealogy in **46:8–27.**

2. Study the material in the Study Guide and in the Leaders Notes. Select those portions of Scripture that are important to read and choose the discussion questions you wish to emphasize.

3. Display the Genesis Family Tree at the back of this book.

4. Plan today's worship.

Before the Session Begins

In this session we focus on guilt and how guilt can affect our lives. You might start a sharing time that allows people to discuss guilt and what it can do. Some will be willing to discuss their experiences with guilt, especially if you are willing to do so. Focus on the guilt and its effect in their lives. How does guilt damage and corrupt life? How can forgiveness be a healing experience? This discussion need not go on long. It can serve as background for the discussion under Creation Now.

Opening Worship

Pray, **Gracious Father, for many years the family of Jacob was separated because of his sons' jealousy of Joseph. They had sinned against Joseph, against their father, and against You. But You changed their hearts and led them to repentance, and we see in today's reading a beautiful family reunion. Forgiveness restores the family and brings peace. Give us repentant hearts and then cheer us with the sure promise of Your forgiveness, for Christ's sake. Make us glad to forgive others, especially those in our family. Amen.**

The Class Session

The Introduction will serve as a lead from your opening discussion into the study of the text. The Overview would be used best as a summary after you have gone through the biblical material. The chapters are too long to read aloud. You might tell the story using the following outline, reading certain parts that emphasize the experience of the people involved.

a. **42:1–23:** Joseph's brothers go to Egypt to buy grain. Joseph recognizes them and accuses them of being spies.

b. **42:25–37:** The brothers return home and tell of the requirement that Benjamin return with them. Jacob refuses.

c. **43:1–34:** Jacob relents; the brothers return to Egypt and are treated royally by Joseph.

d. **44:1–17:** Returning home, they are arrested and taken back, accused of stealing a cup. Benjamin is to be kept as a slave.

e. **44:18–34:** Judah pleads for Benjamin and his father.

f. **45:1–15:** Joseph reveals himself, and there is a warm reunion.

g. **46:1–7:** Jacob goes to Egypt with his family and is promised by God that his descendants will return.

h. **46:8–26:** Genealogy of the family who went to Egypt.

i. **46:28–47:12:** Jacob and Joseph are reunited, and the family is established in Egypt.

j. **47:13–25:** Joseph rules Egypt.

Focus 1: Roots

1. God promises that Jacob's descendants would be able to return to the Promised Land. It is part of the covenant, and it would not be set aside by the action of Jacob and his family. Again, God reveals Himself as both caring and steadfast. He cares for Jacob and gives him this comforting revelation at a time when the move to Egypt must have been difficult. Jacob is again assured that God will not forsake His promises.

2. The statement about the two brothers shows a remarkable change. They are no longer involved in petty jealousy, but they are willing to sacrifice themselves for the good of their father and the others.

Focus 2: Relationships

1. Joseph is very cautious about his relationship to his brothers. He apparently wants to protect himself from being hurt. He also wants to find out if they have changed in their attitude toward him, his father, and his brother Benjamin. He is pleased with them and offers them his trust. God does not "test" us before he trusts us with the revelation of His love in Jesus. It is a free gift. We may reject it, but it is freely offered. On the other hand, there are many ways we test people before we trust them. We are often cautious and careful about others before we reveal ourselves to them. Ideally, Christians who share a common faith in Christ and trust in Him for forgiveness would be more ready to trust each other. Unfortunately, we are not always able to live up to the ideal.

2. Jacob shows some of the signs of the pettiness that plagued him all of his life. His words must have cut his sons very deeply. There is a weakness in all of us, dating back to Adam and Eve, that makes it easier for us to blame someone else than to take responsibility for our actions.

3. The passages tell of a beautiful reunion. Help the class share that joy by recalling some of their times of happy reunion. Talk about heaven and the promise of eternal life in terms of reunion. Sometimes heaven seems sterile and meaningless. We tend to see most value and joy in events that are centered on, and shared by, those we love.

Creation Now

The material here gives you the opportunity to continue your discussion on guilt, its effects, and how it can be dealt with by the Christian.

Guilt is destructive. It breaks down our attitude toward ourselves, our relationship to God, and our relationships to other people. Allow time for members of the class to share some of their experiences (even from childhood) in which they were involved in the destructiveness of guilt.

Stress that there is a real guilt (like the brothers') that comes from a particular act. Often that guilt must be confessed to the person who was hurt by the act.

There is also a false guilt. It is a bad feeling about ourselves, a feeling of worthlessness. That kind of feeling can be destructive. Talk about ways to help and encourage people who suffer from that kind of guilt. It is a difficult thing to deal with. People who hate themselves require much love, care, forgiveness, and the assurance that God is the heavenly Father who loves them and wants to be with them forever.

In every case, when we deal with guilt, we must remember and also remind others that Christ took upon Himself all our guilt when He died on the cross. End the class on the positive assurance that we are truly forgiven and loved in Christ.

Closing Worship

Sing or speak these stanzas from "Chief of Sinners Though I Be."

Chief of sinners though I be,
Jesus shed His blood for me,
Died that I might live on high,
Lives that I might never die.
As the branch is to the vine,
I am His, and He is mine.

Only Jesus can impart
Balm to heal the wounded heart,
Peace that flows from sin forgiv'n,
Joy that lifts the soul to heav'n,
Faith and hope to walk with God
In the way that Enoch trod.

Lesson 13

An End That Is a Beginning
(Genesis 47:29–50:26)

Preparation for This Lesson

1. Read **Gen. 47:29–50:26.** Use your commentary to check anything that is unclear to you.

2. Study the material in the Study Guide and in the Leaders Notes. Decide on which of the discussion questions you will concentrate. Try to choose several in addition to the one under Creation Now that relate the message of the new beginning to us personally.

3. Display the Genesis Family Tree at the back of this book.

4. Plan today's worship or choose a worship leader.

Before the Session Begins

Spend a few minutes looking at the Genesis Family Tree. Concentrate on the truth that even though we have come to the end of the book of **Genesis,** the tree does not stop growing. Mark again those people in the tree who are ancestors of Christ. Focus on the promise of the Messiah to come.

Talk about the end of the class. Does the fact that we are coming to the end of this study produce any special thoughts or feelings in the members of the group? If close relationships have developed, there may be some sadness and thoughts that some things have not been completed.

Opening Worship

Pray, **Dear Father in heaven, today we end this study of Genesis. As You were with Adam and Eve in the beginning, so were You still with Jacob and Joseph at the end of their lives. We know that You kept Your covenant promises to these believers of old, and we are confident that You do the same for us. Thank You for the guidance of the Holy Spirit in our study and for strengthening our faith through the power of Your Word. Make us glad hearers and doers of that Word so that in everything we give glory to Your name. Amen.**

The Class Session

Read the Introduction and the Overview. Concentrate on the feelings experienced by the people in the account. Read the portions of Scripture that you have chosen, or those that seem to be important to the members of the group. A discussion about grief, which might arise out of the Introduction, can be completed under Creation Now.

Focus 1: Roots—New Beginnings

1. The entire structure of the nation of Israel was centered on the 12 tribes. Much of the Hebrew identity was rooted in the tribes. The number 12 carries into the new beginning of the church of Jesus Christ in that He chose 12 disciples. The number is also significant in the book of **Revelation** as a sign of the believers.

2. The great saving act of God to His people of Israel was the exodus. In that act of rescue He formed them into a nation, gave them the rules and laws that shaped their life and worship, and brought them to the Promised Land. The exodus points to Jesus. Through the death and resurrection of Jesus we are called out of the slavery of sin, formed into the people of God in His kingdom (the church), and given the promise of heaven.

3. The words to Judah in **49:8–10** point directly to the "scepter" of Judah—King David. But the promise of the Messiah is also tied closely to the reign of David. The promise to David of a king to rule forever **(Psalm 110)** ties David directly to his Lord—the Messiah.

Focus 2: Relationships

1. The fact that in several cases (Abraham to Isaac, Isaac to Jacob, Jacob to Ephraim and to Judah) the birthright and blessing were given to younger sons emphasizes the hand of God in the choosing. Read also **1 Sam. 16:1–13.** David is also chosen by God in an "out of the ordinary" manner. God chooses according to His plan, not according to the world's rules. He chose us because of His love in Christ, not because of something we have done.

2. In both cases the vow had to do with God's promise of Canaan. To both men, the land was a part of their identity—it was their root. Though the promise of God to us is for a "new kingdom" in heaven with Him, we can experience some of the longing and the belonging that the patriarchs felt for their Promised Land.

3. The purpose of the discussion is how we can respond to the sins of others in the spirit of forgiveness in Christ. It is true, and remains clear in **Genesis,** that sin is a violation of the will of God. We may not excuse it. But in dealing with others who have sinned against us, we are to forgive as God forgives us and as Joseph forgave his brothers. We are commanded to do so **(Matt. 18:21–22).**

Creation Now

In your discussion of grief, be sensitive to any in the class who may have recently experienced the loss of a loved one. You will have to decide if the persons are able to discuss their grief.

Try to emphasize the following points:

a. Grief is normal. It is not a denial of faith in God or the resurrection to grieve over a loved one. It does not demonstrate a lack of faith. Separation always causes pain. We need not feel guilty about it or try to deny our feelings of sorrow, even anger. Denial of those powerful feelings can be destructive.

b. Grief is a process that does come to an end. It does not last forever. It usually moves from denial, to sadness, to depression, to healing. It is important to emphasize that people need our support and comfort—our "weeping with them" for a longer period of time than just the first few days. The grief process may continue for weeks or months or years, but it does end. If it does not, professional help should be sought.

c. We have the message of the resurrection to give us strength in the face of our own death and to give comfort at the death of a loved one. Point out that comforting others with the resurrection promise is not just saying the words when someone is grieving. The comforting, like the grieving, is a process that means joining in the sorrow of the person and helping him or her see the message of hope in the resurrection. Sometimes the sadness and anger get in the way. It is our task to stay with the grieving until the promise of the resurrection can be heard.

Keep the discussion positive and hopeful. Joseph's and Jacob's stories did not end in the grave—neither does the book of **Genesis** end in the grave. The grave is an entrance to a new beginning, and our death also is an entrance to new life in heaven.

Closing Worship

Sing or speak these stanzas from "Glory Be to God the Father."

Glory be to God the Father,
Glory be to God the Son,
Glory be to God the Spirit:
Great Jehovah, Three in One!
Glory, glory While eternal ages run!

Glory, blessing, praise eternal!
Thus the choir of angels sings;
Honor, riches, pow'r, dominion!
Thus its praise creation brings.
Glory, glory, glory to the King of kings!

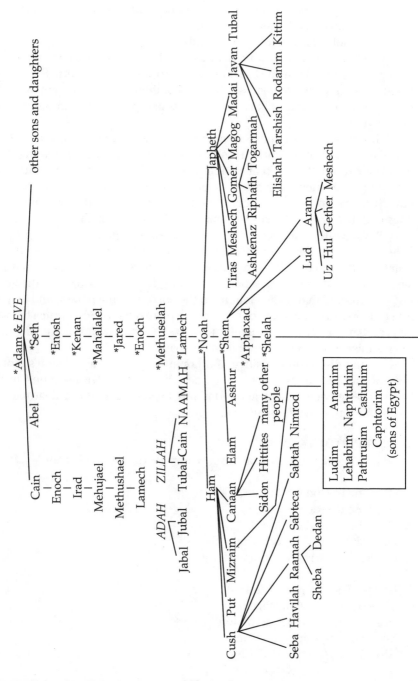

other sons and daughters

*Adam & EVE

*Seth
*Enosh
*Kenan
*Mahalalel
*Jared
*Enoch
*Methuselah
*Lamech
*Noah
*Shem
*Arphaxad
*Shelah

Cain
Abel

Enoch
Irad
Mehujael
Methushael
Lamech

ADAH   ZILLAH
Jabal Jubal   Tubal-Cain NAAMAH

Japheth
Tiras Meshech Gomer Magog Madai Javan Tubal
Ashkenaz Riphath Togarmah
Elishah Tarshish Rodanim Kittim

Lud Aram
Uz Hul Gether Meshech

Shem
Asshur
Elam

Ham
Cush Put Mizraim Canaan
Sidon Hittites many other people

Cush
Seba Havilah Raamah Sabteca
Sheba Dedan
Sabtah Nimrod

Ludim   Anamim
Lehabim Naphtuhim
Pathrusim Casluhim
Caphtorim
(sons of Egypt)

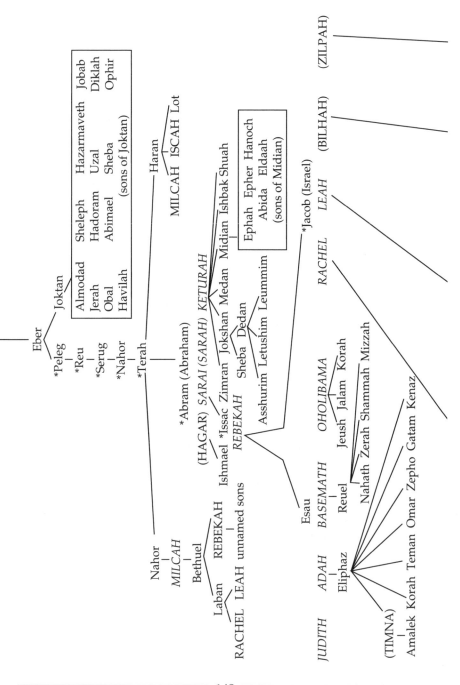

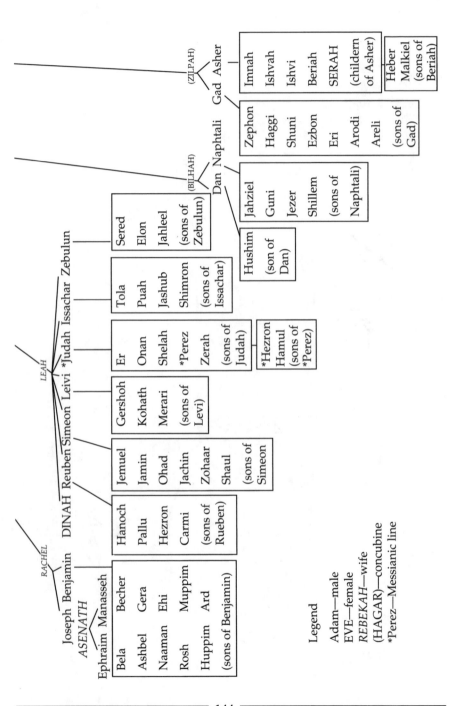

Legend

Adam—male
EVE—female
REBEKAH—wife
(HAGAR)—concubine
*Perez—Messianic line